MARXIST LIBRARY

Works of Marxism-Leninism
Letters to Dr. Kugelmann

MARXIST LIBRARY
Works of Marxism – Leninism
VOLUME XVII

LETTERS TO DR. KUGELMANN

By
KARL MARX

NEW YORK
INTERNATIONAL PUBLISHERS

First Published by Cooperative Publishing
Society of Foreign Workers in the U.S.S.R.

Printed in the Union of Soviet Socialist Republics

CONTENTS

FOREWORD

Marx's letters to Kugelmann appear here for the first time in the English language. The translation is based on the original text of the letters, the complete collection of which is to be found in the Marx-Engels-Lenin Institute in Moscow.

The recipient of the letters, Dr. L. Kugelmann (1830-1902), was a surgeon and gynæcologist with a large practice in Hanover, who in his youth took part in the revolutionary movement of 1848 and who throughout his life regarded himself as an ardent follower of Marx. The study of Marx's *Eighteenth Brumaire* (1852) and *The Critique of Political Economy* (1850) caused him to desire to make the acquaintance of Marx. This he succeeded in doing in 1862, through the aid of the German poet, Freiligrath, who at that time was living in London as a political emigrant. The acquaintance, first begun by correspondence (see the first letter in the series), soon ripened into an intimate friendship. As is evident from the correspondence, Kugelmann was able to render Marx some very valuable services by keeping him informed on German affairs, and by securing publicity for *Capital*. He was member of the First International and attended the Congresses, at Lausanne (1867) and the Hague (1872) as a delegate.

The friendly relations between Marx and Kugelmann came to an end in 1874 when both were staying at Karlsbad. Although calling himself a Marxist, Kugelmann never really understood Marxism or fully grasped the revolutionary essence of Marx's teaching. While admiring and even worshipping Marx the thinker, the man of science and genius, Kugelmann could not reconcile himself to Marx the revolutionary, the leader and organiser of the revolutionary proletariat and its party. Although a sincere believer in the ultimate triumph of socialism, he rejected the proletarian class struggle and expected the realisation of his ideal in a purely reformist way. These views of Kugelmann could

9

not but lead to an estrangement and even to a rupture between the two.

Even after the rupture Kugelmann continued in his *"cultus"* of Marx, kept on inquiring about him of some of the members of Marx's family and of Engels, and continued his propaganda for *Capital*. He cherished Marx's letters as the "greatest pride of his life" and urged the leaders of German Social-Democracy to publish them after his death.

Kautsky published the letters in 1902 in the *Neue Zeit*, the theoretical organ of the German Social-Democratic Party at that time. The two letters on the Paris Commune (April 12 and 17, 1871) attracted the special attention of Lenin and prompted him to undertake the publication of these letters in Russian. In his Introduction written in 1907 and reprinted here, Lenin lays special stress on these letters and contrasts Marx's revolutionary attitude to the Paris Commune with the cowardly opportunist attitude of Plekhanov to the December uprising of 1905 in Moscow.

In his edition, Kautsky omitted several passages, mostly of a personal nature, but of great value for the study of the life of Marx. Moreover, out of opportunist considerations, he entirely suppressed the letter of February 23, 1865. This letter, the third in the series, contains an extremely severe criticism of Lassalle and of opportunism generally, the so-called "real politics," which Marx unmasks as a reactionary, treacherous policy which regards "as reality" only "the interest immediately in front of" its "nose . . . whereas, in the very nature of the case, the working class must be sincerely revolutionary." This letter was still unknown to Lenin in 1907 when he wrote his Preface.

Marx-Engels-Lenin Institute.

PREFACE
TO THE RUSSIAN TRANSLATION OF MARX'S LETTERS TO KUGELMANN

By V. I. Lenin

Our aim in publishing in a separate pamphlet the full collection of Marx's *Letters to Kugelmann* that were published in the German Social-Democratic weekly, the *Neue Zeit,* is to acquaint the Russian public more closely with Marx and Marxism. As was to be expected, Marx devoted a good deal of space in the correspondence to personal matters. This material is exceedingly valuable for the biographer. But for the general public, and the Russian working class in particular, those passages which contain theoretical and political material are of infinitely greater interest. It is particularly important and instructive for us in our present revolutionary times to consider carefully this material, which reveals Marx as a man who immediately responded to all questions on the labour movement and world politics. The editor of the *Neue Zeit* was quite right when he remarked that "we are elevated by an acquaintance with the personality of men whose thoughts and will took shape in conditions of grave upheavals." For the Russian Socialist in 1907, acquaintance with this material is doubly necessary, for it provides a wealth of very valuable indications concerning the immediate problems confronting the Socialist in all and every revolution his country is passing through. Just now Russia is passing through a "great upheaval." The policy Marx pursued in the comparatively stormy period of the 1860's should very often serve as a model of the policy a Social-Democrat should pursue in the present Russian revolution.

We will therefore very briefly note the passages in Marx's correspondence which are particularly important from a theoretical point of view and we will deal in greater detail with his revolutionary policy as a representative of the proletariat.

Of outstanding interest from the point of view of a fuller and

more profound elucidation of Marxism is the letter of July 11,
1868. In this letter, Marx, in the form of polemical remarks
against the vulgar economists, very clearly expounds *his* conception of the so-called "labour" theory of value. The very objections to Marx's theory of value which naturally arise in the
minds of the less-trained readers of *Capital* and which are for
that reason more eagerly seized upon by the mediocre representatives of "professorial" bourgeois "science" are here analysed
by Marx briefly, simply and with remarkable lucidity. Marx shows
the way in which he proceeded, and the way one should proceed
to arrive at an explanation of the law of value. By quoting exam-
ples of the most common objections he teaches us his *method*.
He makes clear the connection between such a purely (it would
seem) theoretical and abstract question as the theory of value
and "the interests of the ruling classes," which require the *"per-
petuation of confusion."* It is to be hoped that everyone who begins to study Marx and to read his *Capital* will read and re-read
this letter when studying the first and more difficult chapters of
Capital.

The other passages in the letters which are particularly interesting from the theoretical point of view are those in which Marx
gives an estimation of various writers. Reading these opinions of
Marx, vividly written, full of passion and displaying an all-
embracing interest in all great ideological trends and in the analysis of these trends—reading these one feels that one is listening
to the utterances of a thinker of genius. Besides his casual opinions of Dietzgen, those on the Proudhonists deserve the special
attention of the reader. The "brilliant" intellectual youth of the
bourgeoisie which throws itself "among the proletariat" in periods of social upheaval, which is incapable of acquiring the
point of view of the working class and of carrying on persistent
and serious work among the "rank and file" of proletarian organisations, is depicted by a few strokes with remarkable vivid-
ness.

Here we have an opinion of Dühring, as if in anticipation of
the famous *Anti-Dühring* which Engels (in collaboration with
Marx) wrote nine years later. There is a Russian translation of
this book by Zederbaum which unfortunately contains not only

omissions but also mistakes, and is simply a bad translation.
Here also is an estimation of Thünen touching simultaneously on
Ricardo's theory of rent. Already in 1868, Marx had emphatically
rejected "the mistakes of Ricardo," which he finally refuted in
Volume III of *Capital* published in 1894, but which even today
are repeated by the revisionists—from our ultra-bourgeois and
even "Black Hundred" Mr. Bulgakov to the "almost orthodox"
Maslov.

Of interest also is Marx's opinion of Büchner and his estimation of vulgar materialism and the "superficial twaddle" copied
from Lange (the common source of "professorial" bourgeois philosophy!).

We will now pass to Marx's revolutionary policy. In Russia a
certain petty-bourgeois conception of Marxism finds surprisingly
wide currency among Social-Democrats, the conception that a
revolutionary period with special forms of struggle and special
proletarian problems is almost an anomaly, while a "constitution" and an "extreme opposition" is the rule. In no other country in the world at this moment is there such a profound revolutionary crisis as there is in Russia and in no other country are
there "Marxists" who (belittling and vulgarising Marxism) take
up such a sceptical and philistine attitude towards the revolution.
From the fact that in essence the revolution is a bourgeois revolution they draw the shallow conclusion that the bourgeoisie is the
driving force of the revolution, that the tasks of the proletariat
in this revolution are of an auxiliary and non-independent nature,
that the proletarian leadership of this revolution is impossible!

How excellently this shallow interpretation of Marxism is exposed by Marx in his letters to Kugelmann! Here is a letter dated
April 6, 1866. At that time Marx had finished his principal work.
Fourteen years before he wrote this letter he had already made
his final estimation of the German Revolution of 1848. In 1850
he had himself refuted his own socialistic illusions of an impending socialist revolution in 1848. And in 1866, when only just beginning to observe the growth of new political crises, he writes:

"Will our philistines" (he has in mind the German liberal bourgeoisie)
"at last realise that without a revolution which removes the Hapsburgs and
Hohenzollerns...there must finally come another Thirty Years' War...."

Not a shadow of illusion that the impending revolution (it happened from above and not, as Marx expected, from below) would abolish the bourgeoisie and capitalism. It is a very clear and precise statement that it would only put aside the Prussian and Austrian monarchies. And what faith in this bourgeois revolution! What revolutionary passion of a proletarian warrior who realises the significance bourgeois revolution has for the advancement of the socialist movement!

Three years later, on the eve of the downfall of the Napoleonic Empire in France, Marx noted "a very interesting" social movement and in a *positive outburst of enthusiasm*, he says:

"The Parisians are making a regular study of their recent revolutionary past, in order to prepare themselves for the business of the impending new revolution."

And describing the past struggle of classes which revealed itself in this study, Marx concludes:

"And so the whole historic witches' cauldron is bubbling. When shall we" (in Germany) "be so far!"

Here is a lesson that should be learned by the Russian intellectual Marxists, weakened by scepticism, sunk into torpor by pedantry, inclined to make penitent speeches, rapidly tiring of revolution, longing as for a holiday for the funeral of the revolution and its replacement by constitutional prose. They ought to learn from the theoretician and leader of the proletarians to have faith in the revolution, to acquire ability in rousing the working class to uphold their immediate revolutionary aims to the last, to acquire firmness of spirit which admits of no faint-hearted whimpering because of temporary setbacks to the revolution.

The pedants of Marxism think that this is all ethical twaddle, romance and lack of the sense of realism! No, gentlemen, this is the unification of revolutionary theory and revolutionary politics without which Marxism becomes Brentanoism, Struvism and Sombartism. The teachings of Marx have bound the theory and practice of the class struggle into one inseparable whole. And he who distorts a theory which soberly presents the objective position into a justification of what now exists and who strives to adapt himself as quickly as possible to every temporary ebb in the tide of revolution, to throw off as quickly as possible "revolutionary illusions" and to turn to "realistic" tinkering, is no Marxist.

During the most peaceful, seemingly "idyllic" (as Marx put it) and "hopelessly stick in the mud" (as the *Neue Zeit* put it) times, Marx was able to sense the approach of the revolution and to *rouse* the proletariat to the consciousness of its advanced, revolutionary tasks. Our Russian intellectuals, however, like philistines, vulgarise Marx, and in most revolutionary times teach the proletariat a policy of passivity, of submissively "drifting with the stream," of timidly supporting the most unstable elements of the fashionable liberal party!

Marx's estimation of the Commune is the crowning glory of the *Letters to Kugelmann*. And this estimation becomes particularly valuable when compared with the methods of the Right-wing Russian Social-Democrats. Plekhanov, who, after December 1905, faint-heartedly exclaimed: "They should not have resorted to arms," had the modesty to compare himself to Marx. Marx, he hinted, also put the brakes on the revolution in 1870.

Yes, Marx *too* put the brakes on the revolution. But see what a gulf is opened up between Plekhanov and Marx when this comparison (which Plekhanov himself makes) is made!

In November 1905, a month before the first revolutionary wave reached its culminating point, Plekhanov not only refrained from emphatically warning the Russian proletariat, but on the contrary spoke very definitely about the necessity to *"learn to use arms and to arm."* A month afterwards, however, when the struggle flared up, Plekhanov, without making the slightest attempt to analyse its significance and its role in the general march of events and its connection with the previous forms of struggle, hastened to play the part of a penitent intellectual and exclaimed: "They should not have resorted to arms."

In September 1870, six months before the Commune, Marx emphatically warned the French workers, any attempt at upsetting the new government would be desperate folly, he said in his well-known Address of the International. He revealed *in advance* the nationalistic illusions concerning the possibility of a movement in the spirit of 1792. He had the priscience to say, *not after the event,* but many months before: "Don't resort to arms."

And what was his attitude when this *hopeless cause* (according to his own September declaration) began to be realised in March

1871? Did he merely take the opportunity (as Plekhanov did in regard to the December events) to "have a dig" at his enemies, the Proudhonists and Blanquists who were leading the Commune? Did he, like a scolding school-mistress, say: "I told you so, I warned you, see what you got for your romanticism, your revolutionary ravings"? Did he preach to the Communards, as Plekhanov did to the December fighters, the sermon of the smug philistine: "They should not have resorted to arms"?

No. On April 12, 1871, Marx writes an *enthusiastic* letter to Kugelmann—a letter which we would gladly see hung on the wall of the home of every Russian Social-Democrat and of every literate Russian worker.

In September 1870 Marx called the insurrection desperate folly, but in April 1871, when he saw the mass movement of the people, he treated it with the great attention of a man participating in great events which marked a step forward in the world historical revolutionary movement.

This is an *attempt*, he says, to destroy the bureaucratic military machine and not simply to place it in other hands. And he sings a veritable *hosanna* to the *"heroic"* Paris workers led by the Proudhonists and Blanquists.

"What elasticity," he writes, "what historical initiative, what a capacity for sacrifice in these Parisians. . . . History has no like example of a like greatness."

The historical initiative of the masses is what Marx values above everything. Ah, if only our Russian Social-Democrats would learn from Marx how to appreciate the *historical initiative* the Russian workers and peasants displayed in October and December 1905!

The homage paid to the *historical initiative* of the masses by this profound thinker who foresaw failure six months ahead—and the lifeless, soulless pedantic: "They should not have resorted to arms!" Are these not as far apart as heaven is from earth?

And like a *participant* in the mass struggle to which he reacted with all his characteristic ardour and passion, Marx, while in exile in London, sets to work to criticise the *immediate steps of* the "foolishly brave" Parisians who were *ready to "storm heaven."*

Oh, how our present "realist" wiseacres among the Marxists, who are deriding revolutionary romanticism in Russia in 1906-07, would have scoffed at Marx at that time! How they would have mocked at the *materialist and economist,* the enemy of utopia, who pays homage to an "attempt" to "storm heaven"!

What a flood of tears these "men in mufflers" * would have shed, what condescending smiles or commiseration they would have bestowed upon him for his rebel tendencies, utopianism, etc., etc., and for his estimation of this heaven-storming movement!

But Marx was not filled with the wisdom of these gudgeons who are afraid to discuss the *technique* of the higher forms of revolutionary struggle. It was precisely the *technical* questions of the insurrection that he discussed. Defence or attack? he asks, as if the military operations were taking place outside of London, and he decides that it must be attack: *"They should have marched at once on Versailles. . . ."*

This was written in April 1871, a few weeks before the great and bloody days of May. . . .

The insurgents who began the "desperately foolish" (September 1870) business of storming heaven "should have marched at once on Versailles."

In December 1905, "they should not have resorted to arms" in order to oppose by force the first attempts to take back the liberties that had been won. . . .

No, it is not for nothing that Plekhanov compared himself to Marx!

The "second mistake," continues Marx in his *technical* criticism, was that "the Central Committee" (the *military leadership—note,* this refers to the Central Committee of the National Guard) "surrendered its power *too soon.*"

Marx was able to warn the *leaders* against a premature rising. But his attitude towards the *proletariat* which was storming

* A character in one of Chekhov's stories who was always muffled up in all weathers and who on hearing of some proposed liberal reform would exclaim: "I do hope nothing bad will come of it." —*Ed.*

heaven was that of a practical adviser, that of a participant in
the *struggle* of the masses who were carrying the *whole* movement
to a *higher stage* in spite of the false theories of Blanqui and
Proudhon.

"However that may be," he writes, "the present rising in Paris, even if
it be crushed by the wolves, swine and vile curs of the old society—is the
most glorious deed of our Party since the June insurrection. . . ."

And Marx, without concealing from the proletariat a single
mistake committed by the Commune, dedicated to this *exploit* a
work which *to this very day* serves as the best guide in the struggle for "heaven" and as a terrible bugbear for the liberal and
radical "swine."

Plekhanov dedicated to December a "work" which has almost
become the bible of the Cadets.*

No, it is not for nothing that Plekhanov compared himself to
Marx.

Apparently Kugelmann replied to Marx with some expressions
of doubt and pointed out the hopelessness of the business and
compared realism with romanticism—at least he compared the
Commune, the insurrection, with the peaceful demonstration in
Paris on June 13, 1849.

Immediately Marx reads Kugelmann a severe lecture (letter of
April 17, 1871). He writes:

"World history would, indeed, be very easy to make, if the struggle were
taken up only on condition of infallibly favourable chances."

In September 1870 Marx called the insurrection desperate folly.
But when the *masses* rose Marx wanted to march with them, to
learn with them in the process of the struggle and not to give
them bureaucratic admonitions. He realised that it would be
quackery or hopeless pedantry to attempt to calculate the chances
in advance *with complete accuracy*. *Above everything else* he put
the fact that the working class heroically, self-sacrificingly and
taking the initiative itself, *makes* world history. Marx looked
upon this history from the point of view of those who *make* it
without being able to calculate *exactly* the chances beforehand
and not from the point of view of a moralising intellectual and

---

* The abbreviated title of the Constitutional-Democratic Party.—*Ed.*

philistine who says: "It was easy to foresee . . . they should not have resorted to. . . ."

Marx was able to appreciate the fact that moments occurred in history when the desperate struggle of the *masses* even for a hopeless cause is *necessary* for the sake of the further education of these masses and their training for the *next* struggle.

To our present quasi-Marxists who love to quote Marx merely for the purpose of learning to estimate the past and not to acquire the ability to mould the future—to them such a *method of presenting* the question is incomprehensible and even alien in principle. This did not even occur to Plekhanov when he began to "put the brake on," after December 1905.

But it is precisely this question that Marx raises without in the least forgetting that he himself in September 1870 regarded the insurrection as desperate folly.

"The bourgeois *canaille* of Versailles," he writes, "presented the Parisians with the alternative of taking up the fight or succumbing without a struggle. In the latter case, the *demoralisation of the working class* would have been a *far greater* misfortune than the fall of any number of 'leaders.'"

And with this we shall conclude our brief review of the lessons in a policy worthy of the proletariat which Marx gives in his *Letters to Kugelmann*.

The working class of Russia has already proved and will prove many times again that it is capable of "storming heaven."

February 1907.

LETTERS TO DR. KUGELMANN

LETTERS TO DR. L. KUGELMANN
By KARL MARX

December 28, 1862.

London, 9 Grafton Terrace,
Maitland Park, Haverstock Hill.

Dear Sir,

Some time ago Freiligrath let me have a letter that he received from you. I would have answered sooner, had not a series of misfortunes in my family made it impossible for me to write for some time.

I was very glad to learn from your letter that you and your friends take so warm an interest in my *Critique of Political Economy*. The second part is at last finished, apart from making a fair copy in the final polishing for the press. It will be about thirty printed sheets. It is actually a continuation of Part I, but will appear independently under the title *Capital,* with *A Contribution to the Critique of Political Economy* only as a subtitle. Really it only deals with those matters which should form the third chapter of the first section, namely, capital in general, and does not therefore include the competition of capitals or the credit system. This volume contains what the English call the principles of political economy. It is the quintessence (together with the first part), and the development of the rest (with the exception perhaps of the relations of different state forms to different economic structures of society) could be easily accomplished by others on the basis thus provided.

The long delay is due to the following causes. First of all, the Vogt scandal in 1860 took up a great deal of my time, because I had to make many investigations into matters which were in themselves of no value, engage in litigation, etc. In 1861, because of the American Civil War, I lost my chief source of income, the *New York Tribune.* My contributions to that paper have been suspended up to the present moment. So I have been, and am, compelled to accept a lot of hackwork to keep myself and my family off the streets. I have even decided to become a "practical man," and was to have taken a position in a railway office early next year. Shall I call it good luck or bad? I did not get the post because of my bad handwriting. So you see I had but little time and peace for theoretical work. It is probable that the same reasons will delay the final preparation of my work for the printers longer than I should wish.

As for the publishers, I shall not in any circumstances give the second volume to Herr Duncker. He received the manuscript for Part I in December 1858 and it appeared in July or August 1859. I have some hope, though it is not very great, that Brockhaus will print the thing. The *conspiration de silence* * with which I am honoured by the German literary mob, whenever they realise that abuse will not settle the matter, will affect the sale of my book unfavourably, apart from the tendency of my works. As soon as the fair copy of the manuscript is ready (I intend to start on that in January 1863), I shall bring it to Germany myself, since it is easier to settle matters with the publishers personally.

There is *every prospect* that as soon as the German edition appears, a French edition will be prepared in Paris. I have absolutely no time to do the French myself, still less as I intend either to write the continuation, that is, the conclusion to my treatment of capital, competition and credit, in German, or else to combine the first two works into one volume for the English public. I do not think that we can count on any effect in Germany before a testimonial is obtained from abroad. It is true that the method of presentation adopted in the first book was in a marked degree non-popular. The reason lay partly in the abstract nature of the subject, the limited space at my disposal, and the purpose of the work. This part can be more easily understood, for it deals with more concrete matters. Scientific attempts to revolutionise a science can never be really popular. But once the scientific foundation is laid, popularisation is easy. Should the times grow more stormy, one could again choose the colours and tints which a popular presentation of *these* subjects would

* Conspiracy of silence.

require. On the other hand, it is true that I had expected the German specialists, from simple decency, not to have ignored my work so completely. And in addition to that, I had the by no means pleasant experience of learning that Party friends in Germany who have studied this science for a long time, and who, *privatim*,* wrote me exaggerated outbursts of approval concerning Part I, made not the slightest effort to write a review or even a notice in any of the journals accessible to them. If that is Party tactics, then I must confess that its secrets are impenetrable to me.

I should be very pleased if you would occasionally write to me on the situation at home. We are obviously approaching a revolution—which I have never doubted since 1850. The first act will include a by no means refreshing repetition of the stupidities of '48-'49. However, that is the way of world history, and one has to take it as it is.

With best wishes for the new year,

Yours,

K. Marx.

* Privately.

November 29, 1864.
1 Modena Villas, Maitland Park,
Haverstock Hill, N. W. London.

Dear Friend,

Today you will receive by post 6 copies of the *Address of the Workingmen's International Association,* which was written by me.* Will you please send a copy with my best wishes to Madame Markheim (Fulda), and also one to Herr Miquel.

The Association, or rather its Committee, is important because the leaders of the London Trades Unions are in it, the same people who prepared such a tremendous reception for Garibaldi,** and who thwarted Palmerston's plan for a war with the United States by "monster meetings" in St. James' Hall. The leaders of the Parisian workers are also connected with it.

During the last few years I have suffered a great deal from ill health (*e.g.,* for the last 14 months from carbuncles). My private circumstances have improved through a legacy which I inherited on the death of my mother.

I think that next year, at last, my book on capital (60 sheets) will be ready for the press.

You will easily understand the reasons why I kept aloof from Lassalle's movement during his lifetime, without my formulating them *en detail.**** That, however, does not prevent me, especially as close friends of his asked me to do so, from defending him after his death against such contemptible riffraff as that bawler Karl Blind.

I am afraid that there will be an Italian-Austrian-French war in early summer or spring next year. That will greatly injure the movement in France and England, which is growing considerably.

I hope to hear from you soon.

Yours very sincerely,

K. MARX.

* The Inaugural Address of the International Workingmen's Association, founded September 28, 1864, at a meeting in St. Martin's Hall, Long Acre, London. Marx was elected a member of the Provisional Committee and was instructed by it to write the Inaugural Address which appeared on November 7.
** Garibaldi visited England in April 1864.
*** In detail.

February 23, 1865.

1 Modena Villas, Maitland Park,
Haverstock Hill, London.

Dear Friend,

I received your very interesting letter yesterday and shall now deal with the separate points you raise.

First of all I shall briefly describe my attitude to Lassalle. During his agitation relations between us were suspended: 1. because of the self-flattering braggadocio to which he added the most shameless plagiarism from my writings, etc.; 2. because I *condemned his political tactics;* 3. because, even *before* he began his agitation, I fully explained and "proved" to him here in this country that direct *socialist* action by the "state of Prussia" was nonsense. In his letters to me (from 1848 to 1863), as in our personal encounters, he always declared himself an adherent of the party which I represent. As soon as he had convinced himself, in London (end of 1862), that he could not play his games *with me* he decided to put himself forward as the "workers'" dictator *against* me and the old party. In spite of all that, I recognised his services as an agitator, although towards the end of his brief life even that agitation appeared to me of a more and more ambiguous character. His sudden death, old friendship, sorrowful letters from the Countess Hatzfeld, indignation over the *cowardly impertinence* of the bourgeois press towards one whom in his lifetime they had so greatly feared, all that induced me to publish a short statement against the wretched Blind, which did not, however, deal with the *content* of Lassalle's actions (Hatzfeld sent the statement to the *Nordstern*).

For the same reasons, and in the hope of being able to remove elements which appeared to me dangerous, Engels and I promised to contribute to the *Sozialdemokrat* * (it has published a translation of the Address and at the editors' request I wrote an article about Proudhon on the death of the latter) and, after Schweitzer had sent us a *satisfactory programme of his editorial work,* we allowed our names to be given out as contributors. A further

* It soon became evident that Schweitzer was continuing the Lassallean policy of supporting Bismarck, and Marx, Engels, and also Liebknecht, publicly withdrew from the paper.

guarantee for us was the presence of *W. Liebknecht* as an un-
official member of the editorial board.

However, it soon became clear—the proofs fell into our hands
—that *Lassalle* had in fact *betrayed* the Party. He had entered
into a formal contract with Bismarck (of course *without having
in his hand any sort of guarantees*). At the end of September
1864 he was to go to Hamburg and there (together with the
crazy Schramm * and the Prussian police spy Marr) *force* Bismarck to annex Schleswig-Holstein, that is, he was to proclaim
its incorporation in the name of the "workers," etc. In return
for which Bismarck promised universal suffrage and a few socialist charlatanries. It is a pity that Lassalle could not play the
comedy through to the end. The hoax would have made him look
damned ridiculous and foolish, and would have put a stop forever to all attempts of that sort.**

Lassalle went astray because he was a *"Realpolitiker"* of
the type of Herr Miquel, but cut on a larger pattern and with bigger aims. (By the bye, I had long ago seen sufficiently far through
Miquel to explain his coming forward by the fact that the *Nationalverein* *** offered an excellent excuse for a petty *Hanoverian* lawyer to make his voice heard outside his own four
walls by all Germany, and thus cause the enhanced "reality" of
himself to react again on the Hanoverian homeland, playing the
"Hanoverian Mirabeau" under Prussian protection.) Just as
Miquel and his present friends snatched at the "new era" inaugurated by the Prussian prince regent, in order to join the

---

* Rudolf Schramm.

** From certain *Reichstag* debates (after 1870) it became evident that
Bismarck and Lassalle had met and exchanged letters. Some years ago the
letters that passed between them were discovered among the secret papers
of the Prussian Home Ministry. They show that Lassalle seriously believed
in the possibility of a "social monarchy" and that he could convince
Bismarck that, without his aid, he would never accomplish the unification
of the German empire. The annexation of Schleswig-Holstein "by the workers" was part of Lassalle's plan for his political alliance with Bismarck.

*** *Nationalverein*—National Union founded in 1859 by that part of
the Prussian bourgeoisie which advocated the unification of all the German
States, except Austria, under the leadership of Prussia. The members of
the *Nationalverein* later founded the National Liberal Party which was
one of the main supports of Bismarck.

Nationalverein * and to fasten on to the "Prussian top," just as they developed their "civic pride" generally under *Prussian protection,* so Lassalle wanted to play the Marquis Posa ** of the proletariat with Phillip II of Uckermark,*** Bismarck acting as intermediary between him and the Prussian kingdom. He only imitated the gentlemen of the *Nationalverein*; but while these invoked the Prussian "reaction" in the interests of the middle class, Lassalle shook hands with Bismarck in the interests of the proletariat. These gentlemen had greater justification than Lassalle, in so far as the bourgeois is accustomed to regard the interest immediately in front of his nose as "reality" and as in fact this class has concluded a compromise everywhere, even with feudalism, whereas, in the very nature of the case, the working class must be sincerely *revolutionary.*

For a theatrically vain nature like Lassalle (who was not, however, to be bribed by paltry trash like office, a mayoralty, etc.), it was a most tempting thought: an act directly on behalf of the proletariat, and executed by Ferdinand Lassalle! He was in fact too ignorant of the real economic conditions attending such an act to be critically true to himself. The German workers, on the other hand, were too "demoralised" by the despicable "practical politics" which had induced the German bourgeoisie to tolerate the reaction of 1849-59 and the stupefying of the people, not to hail such a quack saviour, who promised to get them at one bound into the promised land.

Well, to pick up again the threads broken off above. Hardly was the *Sozialdemokrat* founded than it became clear that old Hatzfeld wanted to execute Lassalle's "testament." Through Wagener (of the *Kreuzzeitung*) she was in touch with Bismarck. She placed the *Arbeiterverein* (*Allgemeinen Deutschen*),**** the *Sozialdemokrat,* etc., at his disposal. The annexation of Schles-

---

* *I.e.,* to conclude a compromise with Bismarck. The government of the prince regent of Prussia had inaugurated a regime slightly more liberal than the black reaction of the previous ten years. The old bourgeois opposition hastened to welcome this "new era" and to accommodate itself to Prussian domination, its militarism and its bureaucracy.

** Marquis Posa is the hero of a play by Schiller; he was convinced that he could persuade the tyrant Phillip II of the justice of his cause.

*** The king of Prussia.

**** General Association of German workers.

wig-Holstein was to be proclaimed in the *Sozialdemokrat*, Bismarck to be recognised in general as patron, etc. The whole pretty plan was *frustrated* because we had Liebknecht in Berlin and on the editorial board of the *Sozialdemokrat*. Although Engels and I were not pleased with the editing of the paper, with its lickspittle cult of Lassalle, its occasional coquetting with Bismarck, etc., it was of course more important not to break publicly with the paper for the time being, in order to thwart old Hatzfeld's intrigues and the complete compromising of the workers' party. We therefore made *bonne mine à mauvais jeu,** although privately we were always writing to the *Sozialdemokrat* that Bismarck must be opposed just as much as the Progressives. We even put up with the intrigues of that affected coxcomb Bernhard Becker—who takes the importance granted him in Lassalle's testament quite seriously—*against the International Workingmen's Association.*

Meanwhile Herr Schweitzer's articles in the *Sozialdemokrat* became more and more Bismarckian. I had written to him earlier, that the Progressives could be *intimidated* on the coalition question, but that the *Prussian government would never* concede the complete abolition of the Combination Laws, because that would involve making a breach in the bureaucracy, would give the workers adult status, would shatter the *Gesindeordnung,*** abolish the flogging regime of the aristocracy in the countryside, etc., etc., which Bismarck would never allow, which was altogether incompatible with the Prussian bureaucratic state. I added that if the Chamber rejected the Combination Laws, the government would have recourse to phrases (such phrases, for example, as that the social question demanded "more throughgoing" measures, etc.) in order to retain them. All this proved to be correct. And what did Herr von Schweitzer do? He wrote an article *for* Bismarck and saved all his heroics for such *infiniment petits**** as Schulze, Faucher, etc.

I think that Schweitzer and Co. have honest intentions, but they are *"Realpolitiker."* They want to accommodate themselves to

---

* To put a good face on the matter.
** Master and Servant Laws.
*** Infinitely small people.

existing circumstances and not surrender this *privilege* of "real politics" to the exclusive use of Herr Miquel and Co. (The latter seem to want to keep for themselves the right of intermixture with the Prussian government.) They know that the workers' press and the workers' movement in Prussia (and therefore in the rest of Germany) exist solely *par la grace de la police.** So they want to take the circumstances as they are, and not irritate the government, just like our *"republican" "real politicians,"* who are willing to "put up with" a Hohenzollern *emperor.*

Since I am not a *"Realpolitiker,"* I have found it necessary to sever all connection with the *Sozialdemokrat* in a public declaration signed by myself and Engels (which you will probably see soon in one paper or another). You will understand at the same time why at the present moment I can do *nothing* in Prussia. The government there has refused point blank to renaturalise me as a Prussian citizen. I should only be allowed to *agitate* there in a form acceptable to Herr v. Bismarck.

I prefer a hundred times over my agitation here through the *International Association.* Its influence on the English proletariat is direct and of the greatest importance. We are making a stir here now on the General Suffrage Question, which of course has a *significance here quite different* from what it has in Prussia.

On the whole the progress of this "Association" is *beyond all expectation,* here, in Paris, in Belgium, Switzerland and Italy. Only in Germany, of course, Lassalle's successors oppose me, in the first place, because they are frantically afraid of losing their importance, and, secondly, because they are aware of my avowed opposition to what the Germans call *Realpolitik.* (It is this sort of reality which places Germany so far behind all civilised countries.)

Since anybody who pays 1 shilling for a card can become a member of the Association; since the French chose this form of individual membership (ditto the Belgians), because the law prevents them from joining us as an association, and since the situation is the same in Germany, I have now decided to ask my friends here and in Germany to form small societies wherever they are—the number of members does not matter—each member of which will take out an English membership card. Since

* By the grace of the police.

the English society is *public,* nothing stands in the way of such procedure, even in France. I would be glad if you too were to get into touch with London in this way in your neighbourhood.

Thank you for the prescription. Curiously enough, the villainous illness had started again three days before it arrived. The prescription therefore was opportune.

I shall send you 24 more copies of the *Address* in a few days.*

I have just been interrupted in my writing by a friend and since I should like to get this letter off, I shall answer the other points in your letter the next time I write.

Yours,

K. M.

---

* Inaugural Address of the First International.

January 15, 1866.
1 Modena Villas,
Haverstock Hill, London.

Dear Friend,

Best wishes for the new year and best thanks for your kind letter.

You must excuse the brevity of these lines because at the moment I am overburdened with work. Next time I shall write more fully.

I am enclosing two cards and in my next letter I shall tell you the questions which are to be dealt with at the public Congress in Geneva at the end of May.

Our Association has made great progress. It already has three official organs: a London one, *The Workman's Advocate*, one at Brussels, *La Tribune du Peuple* * and one for the French Section in Switzerland, *Journal de l'Association Internationale des Travailleurs, Section de la Suisse Romande* ** (Geneva), while a paper for the German Swiss Section, *Der Vorbote*,*** will appear in a few days under the editorship of J. P. Becker (Address: 6 Rue du Mole, Geneva, in case you would like to send him contributions occasionally, political or social).

We have succeeded in drawing into the movement the one really big workers' organisation, the English Trades Unions, which formerly concerned themselves *exclusively* with wage questions. With their help the English Society**** which we founded for achieving universal suffrage (half of its central committee consists of members—workers—of our Central Committee) held a monster meeting a few weeks ago, at which only workers spoke. You can judge of the effect by the fact that the *Times* dealt with the meeting in leading articles in two consecutive issues.

As for my book, I am working twelve hours a day at writing out the fair copy. I think I shall bring the manuscript of the first

* *The People's Tribune.*
** *Journal of the International Workingmen's Association, Latin-Swiss Section.*
*** *The Herald.*
**** The Reform League; household suffrage was granted in 1867.

volume to Hamburg in March, and take the opportunity of seeing you.

The antics of Justus von Möser's successor * amused me very much. How paltry must a man of talent be, who seeks and finds satisfaction in such trifles!

As for Bürgers, he is of course well meaning, but weak. Little more than a year ago he declared at a public meeting in Cologne (see the Cologne newspapers) that Schulze-Delitzsch had definitively "solved" the social question and that he (Bürgers) had only strayed into the Communist maze out of *personal friendship for me!* After such public declarations, could I consider him otherwise than as a "renegade"?

Yours very sincerely,

K. MARX.

---

* This refers to Miquel, who in 1865 became Burgomaster of Osnabrück and member of the Prussian Landtag. Möser also was Burgomaster of Osnabrück.

April 6, 1866.
5 Lansell's Place, Margate.

Dear Friend,

I shall return to London the day after tomorrow. My doctor exiled me to this seaside place, where indeed my health has *greatly improved*. But once again more than two months—February, March, and half of April—have been entirely lost and the completion of my book again postponed. It is enough to drive one mad.

I was suffering from carbuncles, not furuncles. This time it was dangerous. Of course you are right in saying that "dietetic" sins are at the bottom of it. I am too much given to working at night, studying by day and writing by night. That, together with all the worries, private and public, and—so long as I am working hard—the neglect of a regular diet and exercise, etc., is quite enough to disorder the blood.

I received Herr Menke's 100 thalers for the International together with your letter. I have not got the addresses of my French friends in Paris here, but if Herr Menke writes to my friend C. Kaub *(33 Rue des trois Couronnes du Temple)* he can introduce him to V. Schily (German) and Tolain, Fribourg, etc., members of the Paris Committee.

The news from Germany is not very gratifying. Prussia is being pushed by Russia (and Bonaparte), Austria by the latter (following more reluctantly in self-defence). Will our philistines at last realise that without a revolution which removes the Hapsburgs and Hohenzollerns (it is unnecessary to speak of the lesser dung-beetles) there must finally come another Thirty Years' War and a new partition of Germany!

A movement from the Italian side would help Prussia. But if we consider Austria and Prussia in themselves, it is practically certain that the latter would be at a disadvantage, despite all the *Düppel-Rénommage.** In any case Benedek is a better general than Prince Friedrich Karl. Austria could enforce peace on Prussia single-handed, but not Prussia on Austria. Every

---

* Boasting about Düppel, a fortified village in Schleswig captured in 1864 by the Prussians under Prince Friedrich Karl with many prisoners and rich booty.

Prussian success would be an encouragement to Bonaparte to interfere.

While I write these lines to you, Bismarck may have again drawn in his horns. But even that would only postpone the conflict. I think that such a postponement is probable.

This German trouble is a piece of extraordinary good luck for Bonaparte. His position is undermined on all sides. But war would give him a new lease of life.

Write to me soon, and particularly about German affairs.

Yours,

K. M.

London, August 23, 1866.

My Dear Friend,

You must be justly indignant at my long silence, in spite of your many friendly letters. But you will have to excuse me on account of the unusual conditions in which I find myself. As a result of my long illness my economic position has reached a crisis. I have piled up debts which weigh heavily on my mind and make me incapable of doing anything except the work which absorbs me. If I cannot manage to get a loan of at least 1,000 thalers, say at 5 per cent, then I can really see no way out. And in spite of the numerous letters of acknowledgement which I receive from Germany, I don't know where to turn to. I can only make use of the help of private friends, not anything public. You will understand that in such circumstances letter-writing becomes extremely difficult.

I have not yet been able to re-establish my old lucrative connections with America. They are so busy with their own movement over there that any expenditure on European correspondence is considered as *faux frais* * of production. I could remedy that if I myself were to emigrate there, but I consider it my duty to stay in Europe and complete the work which I have been engaged on for so many years.

As far as that work itself is concerned, I don't think that I shall be able to bring the manuscript of the first volume (there will be three) to Hamburg before October. I cannot work productively more than a very few hours a day without feeling the effect physically, and out of consideration for my family I must, however unwillingly, observe hygienic limits until I am completely restored to health. Besides that, my work is often interrupted by adverse external circumstances.

Although I am devoting a great deal of time to the preparations for the Geneva Congress,** I cannot, and do not want to go there, since no such prolonged interruption of my work is possible. I think that this work which I am doing is of far greater

* Incidental expenses.
** The Geneva Congress of the International lasted from September 3 to September 8, 1866.

importance to the working class than anything that I, personally, could do at a Congress *quelconque.**

The international situation in Europe is, I consider, wholly provisional. With regard to Germany in particular, we must take things as we find them, that is, we must utilise revolutionary sentiments in a manner corresponding to the changed circumstances. As to Prussia, it is now more than ever important to watch and to denounce her relations with Russia.

Yours very sincerely,

K. MARX.

---

* Of any sort.

October 9, 1866.

1 Modena Villas, Maitland Park,
Haverstock Hill, London.

Dear Friend,

I hope I have not to conclude from your long silence that my last letter offended you in any way. The very opposite should be the case. In desperate situations, every human being feels the need of unburdening himself to somebody. But he does that only to persons in whom he places particular and exceptional confidence. I assure you that my private affairs make me much more anxious because they hinder the completion of my work than for any personal or family reasons. I could put an end to this state of affairs tomorrow, if I were to follow some practical occupation instead of working for the cause. I hope that you are as little troubled by the fact that *you* cannot help to do away with these troubles. That would be a quite unreasonable reason.

And now for something general. I had great fears for the first Congress at Geneva. On the whole, however, it turned out better than I expected. The effect in France, England and America was unhoped for. I could not, and did not want to go there, but wrote the programme for the London delegation. I deliberately restricted it to those points which allow of immediate agreement and concerted action by the workers and give direct nourishment and impetus to the requirements of the class struggle and the organisation of the workers into a class.* The Parisian gentlemen had their heads full of the emptiest Proudhonist phrases. They babble about science and know nothing. They scorn all *revolutionary* action, *i.e.*, action arising out of the class struggle itself, all concentrated social movements, and therefore all those which can be carried through by *political means*, *e.g.*, the *legal* limitation of the working day.

Under the *pretext of freedom*, and of anti-governmentalism or

---

* The Geneva Congress adopted the General Rules of the International. In addition the Congress carried resolutions on the normal working day, limitation of child labour, introduction of a rational system of education, the necessity of fighting tsarist Russia, the establishment of a democratic Poland, trade unions, co-operation, direct and indirect taxation and standing armies, etc. The Geneva Congress also decided on the collection of labour statistics by the organisations affiliated to the I.W.M.A.

anti-authoritarian-individualism, these gentlemen—who for six-
teen years have so calmly endured the most miserable despotism,
and still endure it—actually preach the ordinary bourgeois science,
only Proudhonistically idealised! Proudhon has done enormous
mischief. His sham criticism and sham opposition to the utopians
(he himself is only a philistine utopian, whereas in the utopias
of a Fourier, an Owen, etc., there is the presentiment and imagin-
ative expression of a new world) attracted and corrupted first the
"brilliant youth," the students, and then the workmen, particularly those of Paris who, as workers in luxury trades, are
strongly attached, without knowing it, to the old muck. Ignorant,
vain, presumptuous, chattering, dogmatic, arrogant, they were on
the point of spoiling everything, for they came to the Congress
in numbers which bore no proportion whatever to the number of
their members. I shall have a dig at them in the report without
mentioning names.

I was very pleased with the American workers' Congress at
Baltimore which took place at the same time. The slogan there
was organisation for the struggle against capital, and curiously
enough, most of the demands which I drew up for Geneva were
also put forward by the correct instinct of the workers.

The Reform movement here, which our Central Council called
into existence *(quorum magna pars fui *)*, has now reached immense and irresistible dimensions. I have kept behind the scenes
all the time and do not trouble myself further about the affair,
since it has been set going.

Yours,

K. Marx.

A propos. The Workman is a philistine paper and has nothing
to do with us. *The Commonwealth* belongs to our people, but at
the moment (partly for economic and partly for political reasons) has become a purely reform organ.

I have recently read Dr. T. Moilin's *Leçons de Médicine Phy-
siologique*** which was published in Paris in 1865. He has
several crotchets and there is too much "construction," but there

---

* Quotation from Virgil's *Æneid: quorum magna pars fui*=in which I
played a great part.
** *Lessons in Physiological Medicine.*

is also a good deal of criticism directed against the old therapeutics. I would like you to read the book and send me your detailed opinion of it. I also recommend to you Tremaux's *De l'origine de tous les êtres, etc.** Although diffusely written, full of geological blunders and greatly deficient in literary-historical criticism, it is still—for all that and all that—an advance on Darwin.

---

* *On the Origin of All Organisms, etc.*

London, Saturday, October 13, 1866.

Dear Friend,

Since I want to answer you at once, and your letter has come just before the post goes (and as tomorrow, Sunday, letters don't go from here) I shall tell you in a few words the quintessence of my intercepted letter. (This interception of letters is anything but pleasant, for I have no desire whatever to make Herr Bismarck the confidant of my private affairs. If, on the other hand, he is anxious to have my opinion of *his* policy, he can apply directly to me and I certainly shan't mince my words.)

My economic position has become so bad as a result of my long illness and the many expenses which it entailed, that I am faced with a financial crisis in the *immediate* future, a thing which, apart from the direct effects on me and my family, would also be disastrous for me politically, particularly here in London, where one must "keep up appearances." What I wanted to ask you was: Do you know anybody, or a few persons (*in no circumstances* must the matter become *public*), who would lend me about 1,000 thalers at 5 or 6 per cent interest for at least two years? I am now paying 20 to 30 per cent interest for the small sums which I borrow, but even so I cannot put off my creditors much longer and I am therefore faced with the break-up of our household.

Since my last letter but one to you, I have again had continual relapses and have therefore been constantly interrupted in my theoretical work (the practical work for the International Association goes on all the time, and there is a great deal of it, for really I have to lead the whole society). Next month I shall send the first sheets to Meissner and continue doing so until I bring the remainder to Hamburg myself. Then I shall visit you, in any case.

My circumstances (physical and external * interruptions without intermission) make it necessary for the first volume to appear separately, not both volumes together, as I had at first intended. There will probably be three volumes after all.

The whole work is divided as follows:

Book I. *The Production Process of Capital*.

* *I.e.*, in consequence of domestic and financial troubles.

Book II. *Circulation Process of Capital.*
Book III. *Form of the Process as a Whole.*
Book IV. *Contribution to the History of Economic Theory.*
The first volume contains the first two books.
The third book will, I think, fill the second volume, and the fourth book the third.

I considered it necessary to begin in the first book *ab ovo*,* that is, to make in one chapter on commodities and money a resume of the book which Duncker published. I thought that necessary not only for the sake of completeness, but also because even people with quite good heads did not grasp the matter quite rightly, and there must therefore be something lacking in the first presentation, particularly in the *analysis of commodities.* Lassalle, for example, in his *Kapital und Arbeit*, where he is supposed to have given the "intellectual quintessence" of my development of the question, makes great blunders, which, it is true, always happens with him in his very unceremonious appropriation of my works. It is funny to hear him accuse me of literary and historical "errors," because I frequently quote from memory, without looking up the original. I have not yet quite made up my mind whether I should put in a few words in the preface about Lassalle's plagiarism. The shameless way in which his blind followers have come out against me would anyway justify my doing so.

The London Council of the English Trades Unions (its secretary is our President, Odger) is just discussing whether it should call itself the British Section of the International Association. If that is done, then in a certain sense we shall have control of the working class here, and we can push on the movement very much.

Salut.

Yours,

K. MARX.

* From the beginning.

London, October 25, 1866.

Dear Friend,

A few lines at once,

1. to thank you for your efforts;

2. to tell you that I received this, as well as the previous letters;

3. you mistake my relations with Engels. He is my most intimate friend. I have *no secrets* from him. Had it not been for him I should long ago have been compelled to take up "business." Therefore in no circumstances do I want any third person to intervene with him on my account. He also, obviously, can only act within certain limits.

4. Dr. Jakobi,* I have been informed by workers, has become a very good citizen and consequently is not to be troubled in any way with my private affairs.

I must see about doing something, but I see that you have tried to do everything in your power, and therefore ask you to consider this affair settled.

I do *not* write for the *Commonwealth*.

Yours,

K. M.

Miquel and Co. can wait a long time before they become Prussian ministers.

K. M.

* Abraham Jakobi.

London, February 18, 1867.

Dear Kugelmann,

Will you see if you can get the following reply inserted in the *Zeitung für Norddeutschland,* and if they refuse it, in another Hanoverian paper. It is important for me because I actually intend to go to Germany in a few weeks' time. The whole notice smells like Stieber.

In a few days I shall send you the official report of the Geneva Congress which is now appearing in serial form, both English and French, in a paper here. The *Commonwealth* is up to its neck in the reform movement. Its editorship is in very bad hands. At the moment we have reasons for letting it go on as it is, although we could intervene as share-holders.

Recently our Society has had all sorts of quarrels with Monsieur Bonaparte. More next time. Please let me know what Liebknecht is doing and where he is.

Yours,

K. MARX.

[The enclosure reads:]
To the Editor of the *Zeitung für Norddeutschland*

It appears to me that the notice published, probably inadvertently, in No. 5522 of your journal: "Dr. Marx, resident in London, seems to have decided upon a journey to the Continent in order to conduct propaganda for this affair (the approaching Polish insurrection)" is a police fabrication hatched for I know not what "affair."
London, February 18, 1867.

[This declaration was not published in full, the Editors of the paper confining themselves to a short note of its contents.]

London, June 10, 1867.

Dear Friend,

The delay in this letter lays me open to the more or less "well-founded" suspicion of being a "rascally fellow." In extenuation I can but say that I have only been "residing" in London a few days. Before that I was with Engels in Manchester. But you and your dear wife know me well enough by now to recognise that letter-writing sins are the normal thing with me. All the same I was with you every day. I count my stay in Hanover among the most beautiful and delightful oases in the desert of life.

I met with no adventures in Hamburg except that, in spite of all precautions, I made the acquaintance of Herr Wilhelm Marr. He is, as far as his personality is concerned, a christian edition of Lassalle, of course of much less value. Also, Herr Niemann was playing during the few days which I spent there. But I was too spoilt by the company in Hanover to want to visit the theatre in less pleasant society. So I missed Herr Niemann.

À propos. Meissner is prepared to print the medical brochure you intend to write. You have only to send him the manuscript and refer to me. As to particulars, you will have to make further arrangements yourself.

Except for rather raw weather on the first day, the journey from Hamburg to London was quite pleasant. A few hours before we reached London a German girl, who had already attracted my attention by her military bearing, announced that she intended to travel from London to Weston-Super-Mare that same evening and did not know how, with all her luggage, she was to set about it. The case was made worse by the fact that on the Sabbath helpful hands are lacking in England. She showed me the name of the railway station in London from which she was to travel. Friends had written it down on a card. It was the North Western station, which I too had to pass. So, like a good knight, I offered to put her down at the station. Accepted. And then it occurred to me that Weston-Super-Mare lies South West, while the station which I had to pass and which had been written down for the young girl was North West. I consulted the captain. And it turned out that she had to go from a part of London lying in a totally different direction from where I wished to go. But I had under-

taken to do it and had to make *bonne mine à mauvais jeu.** We
arrived at 2 in the afternoon. I took the *donna errante*** to the
station, and learnt that her train did not leave until 8 in the
evening. So I was in for it, and had to kill six hours with Mad-
emoiselle by walking in Hyde Park, visiting ice-cream shops, etc.
It turned out that she was called Elizabeth von Puttkammer, a
niece of Bismarck, with whom she had just spent a few weeks in
Berlin. She had the whole Army List with her, for this family
supplies our "brave army" in abundance with gentlemen of honour and good figure. She was a gay, educated girl, but aristo-
cratic and blackwhite *** to the tip of her nose. She was not a
little astonished to learn that she had fallen into "red" hands.
But I assured her that our *rendezvous* would pass "without
bloodshed" and saw her off, *saine et sauve,**** from the station. Just think what fodder my conspiracy with Bismarck would
give to Blind or other vulgar democrats!

Today I sent off the 14th corrected proof sheet. I received most
of these while with Engels, who is extraordinarily pleased with
them and, with the exception of sheets 2 and 3, found them written in a manner *very* easy to understand. His verdict set my mind
at rest, for I find that, when printed, my things always displease
me, especially at first sight.

I am sending your dear wife, to whom I ask you to convey my
special thanks for her friendly and cordial reception, the photograph of my second daughter Laura, since there are no more of
the others left, and new ones will have to be taken. Engels will
also have new copies made of his own and Wolff's photograph.
He was greatly pleased by your despatches.

My best greetings to the *"Madämchen,"***** Eleanor is at
school, otherwise she would write to her. And now, Adio!

Yours,

KARL MARX.

---

* To put a good face on the matter.
** Wandering lady.
*** The Prussian colours.
**** Safe and sound.
***** "Little lady"—Kugelmann's daughter.

London, July 13, 1867.

Dear Friend,

Thanks for Hegel and *Madämchen!*

I shall now answer briefly on all points.

Engels is at present in Denmark and will visit you for one day during the course of this month. *Ad vocem* * Engels: You remember you told me that *Menke* (or whatever the man in your statistical bureau at Hanover is called) expressed great admiration for my book which Duncker published. In speaking to *Engels* I *twisted* this by saying that Menke had expressed to me his great admiration for *Engels' Lage der Arbeitenden Klasse.*** The reason for this pious fraud (and I have committed many such frauds with the *same object* in view) is to *induce* Engels to write and publish the second volume, *from 1845 down to the present day.* I have finally succeeded to the extent of obtaining a promise that he will set about it. So that if by any chance the statistician should be mentioned, don't let the cat out of the bag.

It is undecided and undecidable whether my wife will make the journey, because in the meantime it has been arranged for my three daughters to go to Bordeaux, to Lafargue Senior.

I advise you *not* to go to Paris. Among that Babylon of things and in the midst of that crowd of people it is impossible to study anything, unless you stay at least six weeks, which is *very dear.*

My book runs to about 50 sheets. You see how greatly I miscalculated as to its extent. A few days ago I sent off to Leipzig the *Appendix*, with the title: *The Form of Value*, Appendix to Chapter I, 1. You know the author of this plan, to whom I herewith render thanks for his suggestion.***

Will you excuse me for breaking off here. New proofs have just arrived.

Yours,

K. MARX.

In my next letter I shall send membership cards for Mrs. Kugelmann and Mrs. Tenge. A lady, Mrs. Law, has been promoted to membership of our Central Council. Best thanks from Eleanor for the stamps. Photographs later.

* As to.
** *Conditions of the Working Class in England*, 1844.
*** Kugelmann himself.

Dear Kugelmann,   October 11, 1867.*

D'abord** best thanks for your two letters. It gives me great
pleasure to hear from you as often as your time permits you to
write. Only you must not count upon strict reciprocity, because,
as it is, my time scarcely suffices for the multifarious correspondence I must keep up on all sides.

Before I speak about my book, something immediate, or an
immediate something. I am afraid that Borkheim, *malgré lui,****
is on the point of doing me a very bad turn—he is having his
speech at Geneva printed in four languages, French, German,
English and Russian.**** He has in addition decorated it with
a baroque and tasteless introduction, overladen with quotations.

Between ourselves—and in the interests of the Party—I must
tell you the whole truth. Borkheim is a capable man, and even
an *homme d'ésprit.****** But when he takes up the pen—oh
dear! All tact and taste leave him. And the necessary preliminary
knowledge, too. He is like the savages, who think they beautify
their faces by tattooing them in screaming colours. Banality and
buffoonery always trip him up. Almost every phrase of his instinctively puts on cap and bells. If he were not so thoroughly
vain, I could have prevented the publication and made it clear to
him how lucky he was that they did *not understand* him at Geneva, but only a few good points in his speech. On the other hand,
I owe him my thanks for the part he took in the Vogt affair and
he is my personal friend. In his speech, etc., there are some
phrases in which he repeats my opinions in a form suitable to the
Kladderadatsch.****** It will be a very fine game for my ene-

* On the preceding day Marx had written to Engels: "Kugelmann's en-
closed letter will show you that the moment for action has come. You can
write him about my book much better than I can."
** First of all.
*** In spite of himself.
**** A reference to Borkheim's pamphlet, *My Pearl before the Geneva
Congress.* At the International Peace and Liberty Conference in Geneva
(September 9-12) organised by petty-bourgeois pacifists and supporters of
free trade, which was attended also by Kugelmann, Borkheim attempted to
deliver a speech calling for war on tsarist Russia. The noisy peace advo-
cates prevented him from finishing his speech which he decided to publish
as a pamphlet.
***** Man of wit.
****** The German equivalent of *Punch.*

mies (Vogt has already hinted in the *Neue Züricher Zeitung* that I am the secret author of the speech), instead of attacking my book, to make me responsible for Herr Borkheim, his stupidities and personalities. Should something of that sort happen, you must manage through Warnebold, etc., to get into the papers open to you short articles revealing these tactics and, without insulting Borkheim in any way, say outright that only deliberate malice or the most complete lack of any critical faculty could identify such disparate views. The baroque and confused manner in which our opinions are reflected in Borkheim's head (not when he speaks, but when he writes) naturally offers the common press gang a most welcome pretext for taking the offensive and may even give them the opportunity of indirectly injuring my book.

Should the press, however, be silent on the matter, which I can scarcely hope, since Borkheim has sent his offspring with all due care to all the newspapers, do not *in any way* disturb that *solemn silence*.

Were Borkheim not a personal friend, I would publicly disavow him. You understand my false position and, at the same time, my annoyance. One submits to the public a book worked out with painstaking care (and never perhaps has a work of that kind been written in more difficult circumstances) in order to raise the Party as high as possible and to disarm even the vulgar by the manner of presentation, and, at the same time, a Party member in motley coat and cap and bells thrusts himself to your side on the market and provokes rotten apples and eggs which may hit oneself and the Party!

I am very *satisfait* * with your manœuvres against Vogt ** at Geneva. I am glad that you like my book.

As to your questions:

Ernest Jones had to speak to *Irishmen* in Ireland as a Party man; that is, since large-scale landownership there is identical with *England's property in Ireland*, he had to speak *against* large-scale landownership. You should never look for principles

* Satisfied.
** At the Geneva Conference organised by the League for Peace and Liberty in September 1867, Kugelmann made a speech against Marx's old enemy, K. Vogt.

in the hustings speeches of English politicians, but only for what is expedient for the immediate purpose.

Peonage is the advance of money against future labour. These advances then follow the usual course of usury. The worker not only remains a debtor all his life, that is, the forced labourer of the creditor, but the relation is handed down in the family to later generations, which in fact *belong* to the creditor.

The completion of my second volume depends chiefly upon the success of the first. This is necessary if I am to find a publisher in England and *without that* my miserable material position will remain so difficult and disturbing, that I shall find neither the time nor the peace for rapid completion. These are of course matters which I do *not* want Herr Meissner to know. It therefore depends now on the skill and the activity of my Party friends in Germany whether the second volume takes a long or short time to appear. Genuine criticism—whether from friend or foe—can only be expected in the course of time, for such a comprehensive and to some extent difficult work requires time to read through and digest. But immediate success is the result, not of genuine criticism, but, to put it bluntly, of creating a stir, of beating the drum, which also forces the enemy to speak. To start off it is not very important *what is said. Above all no time should be lost.*

I have sent your last letter to Engels, so that he can let you have the necessary hints. He can write better about my book than I can myself.

My warmest greetings to your dear wife. In a few days I shall send her a prescription for reading the book.

Yours,

K. M.

Keep me *au fait* with everything that happens in Germany in regard to Volume I.

As Paul Stumpf (Mainz) has written me a letter in which he calls Borkheim's speech "my" speech, and as at the moment I have *no time* to write to Stumpf, will you please write and explain to him, recommending silence when Borkheim's pamphlet appears. Between ourselves, Stumpf also becomes a nuisance when he takes up the pen.

October 15, 1867.

Dear Kugelmann,

You must *not* write to Borkheim. Besides it would be use-
less, since the work has already been announced in the publishers' circular and Schabelitz has already brought it out. Moreover, Borkheim himself is now in Bordeaux. Such a letter from
you would have no other effect but to make Borkheim my
enemy.

Ce qui est fait, est fait*—never mind! As I was in a state of
great excitement from working at night, I exaggerated the mal-
ignity of the *événement *** at first. In fact *je suis puni par ou j'ai
peché!**** Actually the idea of the scandal which our friend
would make among the respectable philistines at Geneva amused
me *au premier abord.***** It is true I did not foresee the *publishers' fruits.* Moreover, I should have realised that in working
out his plan Borkheim would naturally overstep the prudent limits I suggested in my letter. The only policy to be pursued now
is *to be silent,* so long as our enemies do not speak, and once they
speak and want to make me responsible, to make bad jokes about
their being compelled to ascribe Borkheim's pranks to me in
order not to have to answer my book. Further, in that event
Borkheim must be dealt with benevolently, for after all, apart
from his literary vanity, he is capable and well meaning, and
good as an *homme d'action,****** as long as he does not get the
devil in him.

You will have received Engels' recipe by now. I am in correspondence with Liebknecht and Becker.******

By "success of the book" I mean nothing but its *rapid sale,*
because of the effect that would have in England.

The *Courier Français* (the daily paper which arouses the most
attention in Paris now) and the *Liberté* in Brussels have published a French translation of my introduction, together with com-
plimentary preambles.

* What is done, is done.
** Event.
*** I am punished by my own sin.
**** At first blush.
***** Man of action.
****** Johann Philip Becker in Geneva.

A certain Natzmer in New York has offered himself as English translator. *Quod non.* *

Liebknecht's speech in Berlin gives me great pleasure. I sent him some instructions from here.

Poor Becker's position is so bad that he is on the point of giving up his entire political and literary activity. How one regrets not being able to help in such circumstances!

Greetings to your dear wife and my little friend, for whose portrait I still have to thank you.

Yours,
K. M.

* Nothing doing.

Dear Kugelmann,   London, November 30, 1867.

The delay in answering you is due to nothing except illness. I have been quite done up for some weeks.

First of all my best thanks for the trouble you have taken. Engels has written (or will write) to Liebknecht. In any case Liebknecht intended (together with Götz, etc.) to demand in the Reichstag an *enquiry into the conditions of the workers.* He wrote to me in this sense and on his request I sent him some Acts of Parliament dealing with the subject. The plan came to grief because the standing orders left no time for it. On one point you can write to Liebknecht better than Engels or I. And that is, that it is in fact his duty to direct attention to my book at *meetings of workers.* If he does not, the Lassalleans will take charge of the affair, and in the wrong way.

Contzen, lecturer at Leipzig University, a pupil and adherent of Roscher, asked *via* Liebknecht for a copy of my book and promised in return a detailed review from his own standpoint. The book was therefore sent him by Meissner. That would make a good beginning.

The printer's error of "Taucher" * instead of "Faucher" in your notice pleased me. Faucher is one of the economic "itinerant preachers."—He cuts no figure at all among the "erudite" German economists like Roscher, Rau, Mohl, etc. It does him too much honour even to name him. That is why I never let him appear as a proper noun, but only as a verb.

Will you tell your wife that the most immediately readable sections are those on "The Working Day," "Co-operation, the Division of Labour and Machinery" and finally "Primitive Accumulation." You will have to give explanations of incomprehensible terminology. On any other doubtful points, I am at your service.

There are the best prospects of a thorough discussion of the book in France (Paris) (in the *Courier Français,* unfortunately a Proudhonist paper!) and even of a translation.

I shall write more as soon as I am better. Meanwhile I hope that you will write frequently. It always has a stimulating effect on me.

Yours,

KARL MARX.

* In German, diver.

London, December 7, 1867.

Dear Kugelmann,

Were there six people of your calibre in Germany, the resistance of the philistine mass and the *conspiration de silence* * of the experts and newspaper crowd would have been so far broken down that at least some serious discussion would have begun. *Mais il faut attendre!* ** In these words lies the whole secret of *Russian policy.* I am enclosing a letter (please return it) from a German-Russian worker (a tanner).*** Engels remarks, quite rightly, that the autodidactic philosophy—pursued by workers themselves—has made great progress in the case of this tanner in comparison with the cobbler Jakob Böhm; also that only "German workers" are capable of such cerebral work.

Borkheim asked me yesterday who had written the article in the *Zukunft* (he is a subscriber). It must come from one of our people, since you had sent him a copy of it. I said *I did not know. Nota bene!* One should not put all one's cards on the table.

My most cordial thanks to your dear wife for the trouble she took in copying the letter. You should not exploit her so much for "surplus labour."

Bucher, as, if I am not mistaken, I have already told you, has himself asked me to be the *economic correspondent of the Royal Prussian Staatszeitung.* So you see that if I *wanted* to make use of such sources, I could do so without the mediation of a third person.

My illness is the old one—nothing dangerous, but troublesome. With best greetings to your dear wife and Fränzchen.

Yours,

K. MARX.

* Conspiracy of silence.
** But it is necessary to wait.
*** Joseph Dietzgen.

[The letter from Joseph Dietzgen to which Marx refers is as follows:]
Dear Sir,

I beg you to allow me, although unknown to you, to express my admiration for the inestimable services which you have rendered by your investigations both for science and especially for the working class. Already in my early youth, when I was able to suspect rather than to understand the extremely rich content of your writings, I was held spellbound by them and I could not refrain from reading and re-reading them until I had made them properly clear to myself. The enthusiasm aroused in me now by the work of yours which has recently been published in Hamburg impels me to what is perhaps the importunate audacity of desiring to assure you of my acknowledgment, admiration and thankfulness. I had studied earlier the *Contribution to the Critique of Political Economy*, Part I, when it appeared in Berlin, with great diligence and I confess that no book, however voluminous, has furnished me with so much new positive knowledge and instruction as this small work. Consequently I have been awaiting the continuation with much impatience. You expressed for the first time in clear, irresistible scientific form what from now on will be the *conscious* tendency of scientific development, *viz.*, the subordination to human consciousness of the previously blind natural force of the social process of production. It is your immortal achievement, most honoured Sir, to have provided the understanding of this tendency, to have assisted the realisation that our production proceeds unguided. For that, time must and will bring you general acknowledgment. Reading between the lines of your work, I see that the presupposition of your deep-rooted economics is a deep-rooted philosophy.

Since the latter has cost me much labour, I cannot suppress the desire to make a short communication to you about *my* scientific efforts, with the acknowledgment that I am only a tanner with an elementary education.

My subject has been, from an early period, a systematic conception of the world; Ludwig Feuerbach showed me the way to it. Much, however, I owe to my own labours, so that I can now say regarding myself: *general things*, the nature of the general or the *"essence of things"* is scientifically clear to me. What 'it remains for me to know are the *particular things*. Since I know individual details of this, I say to myself that to know all is too much for the indvidual.

The foundation of all science lies in knowledge of the thought process. *Thinking means to develop the general from what is given by the senses, from the particular.*

Appearance forms the *necessary* material of thought. It must be present before the essence, the general or the abstract is to be discovered. The understanding of this fact contains the solution of all philosophic riddles. For instance, the question of the beginning and end of the world does not any longer belong to science, if the world can only be the presupposition but not the result of thought or knowledge.

The essence of thought is number. All logical differences are quantitative. All being is a more or less enduring appearing, all *appearance* is a more or less enduring being.

All causes are effects and vice versa. Within a sequence of phenomena, the one *generally* preceding is termed the cause. Of five birds, four, for instance, take to flight in consequence of a shot. Consequently the shot is said to be the cause that four fly off and undauntedness the cause that one remains. But if, on the contrary, one takes to flight and four remain, it is not now the shot but *timidity* that is said to be the cause of the flight. A famous physicist writes: "We are not able to perceive heat itself, we only conclude from phenomena the existence of this natural agent." I, on the contrary, conclude from the imperceptibility of "heat itself" the non-existence of this agent and understand the phenomena or effects of heat as *Materiatur* [something material] from out of which the mind forms the abstract conception heat. If, without confusing ideas, we call what is concrete sensuous matter, then its abstract is *force*. In weighing a bale of goods, the gravitational force is handled by the pound without regard to the matter making up the weight. The hackneyed Büchner says: "Now what I want is facts," but he does not know what he wants; science is not so much concerned with facts as with the *explanations* of facts, not with matter but with forces. Even if in reality force or matter are identical, their distinction, the separation of the particular and the general is still more than justified. "Force cannot be seen." Oh yes, seeing itself and what we see is pure force. It is true that we do not see things "themselves" but only their effects on our eyes. Matter is imperishable, that means only that it is, everywhere and at all times, matter. Matter appears and the phenomena are material. The difference between appearance and essence is only *quantitative*. The power of thought puts together from out of the many—the one; from out of the parts—the whole; from out of the transitory—the imperishable; from out of the accidents—the substance.

Morality. By morality the world understands the regard which a man pays himself and his neighbours with the aim of his own good. Different persons and groups of persons fix the number and degree of these regards differently. Given the group, the power of thought can only separate general from particular right. What is aim? What is means? In regard to abstract human good, all aims are means and in so far the basic statement holds good "the end justifies the means."

If lack of learning did not hinder me, I would write a work on this theme. I believe that I know so much that is new about it.

Pardon me, dear Sir, for presuming to make this claim on your time and attention. I thought to be able to please you by the proof that the philosophy of a manual worker is clearer than the average of our present day philosophy-professors. I would value your approval higher than if some learned academy wished to appoint me as its member.

I close with the assurance once again that I sympathise from the bottom of my heart with your efforts which have a significance far beyond our time. Social development, the struggle for the rule of the working class, interests me more deeply than my own personal affairs. I regret only not to be able to participate more actively. *Allons enfants de la patrie!*[*]

> Joseph Dietzgen, Master of the Vladimir Tannery
> Vassili Ostrov
> St. Petersburg
> 24 October [7 November] 1867.

[*] "Forward, children of the fatherland." The first line of the *Marseillaise*.

London, January 11, 1868.

Dear Kugelmann,

D'abord * my best happy new years to your wife, Fränzchen and yourself. And then my best thanks for the Jupiter and for the interest you display in doing propaganda and fooling the German press. As our friend Weerth, too early dead, used to sing:

> *Es gibt nichts schöneres auf der Welt*
> *Als seine Feinde zu beissen,*
> *Als über alle die plumpen Gesellen*
> *Seine schlechte Witze zu reissen!* **

With all due respect to your medical authority, you have too low an opinion of the English, German and French doctors, whom I have consulted and still consult here, if you think that they cannot distinguish anthrax (carbuncles) from furuncles, particularly here in England—the land of carbuncles, which is actually a proletarian illness.

And even if the doctors could not distinguish between the two, the patient who knows both sorts of horrors, as I do, could do so; for the subjective impression they make is quite different, although, as far as I know, no doctor has as yet succeeded in making an exact theoretical diagnosis of the two. It is only in the last few years that I have been persecuted with the thing. Before that it was a complete stranger to me.

At the moment of writing to you I am not quite better and not yet able to work. Again several weeks lost and not even *pour le roi de Prusse!* ***

The thing that appears most clearly in Herr Dühring's criticism **** is—fear. I should be very glad if you could get for me Dühring's book *Gegen die Verkleinerer Carey's* and von Thünen's *Der isolierte Staat mit Bezug auf die Landwirt-*

---

* First of all.
** "There's nothing nicer in the world
Than foes of his to bite on,
Than all the fellows ponderous
To try his jokes so trite on!"
*** For the King of Prussia.
**** Dühring's review of *Das Kapital* appearing in the *Ergänzungsblätter zur Kenntnis der Gegenwart*, III, 3.

schaft * or something like that (together with a note of the price). Such orders from here take too long.

Finally I would ask you to be good enough to send me about 12 copies of my photograph (only the fullfaced one). About a dozen friends are plaguing me for them.

Enclosed, for Mrs. Kugelmann, the photographs of my eldest daughter Jenny and of Eleanor, who sends her best greetings to Fränzchen.

Ad vocem Liebknecht: Let him play *le petit grand homme.*** for a little while. All that will turn out for the best in the best of all possible worlds.

I had all sorts of personal anecdotes to relate, but shall save them for the next time, when the writing position no longer troubles me.

Salut.
Yours,

K. Marx.

One of my friends here, who dabbles a lot in phrenology, said yesterday when looking at the photograph of your wife: A great deal of wit! So you see, phrenology is not the baseless art which Hegel imagined.

---

* *Against the Belittlers of Carey; The Isolated State in its Relation to Agriculture.*
** The great man in miniature.

London, January 30, 1868.

Dear Kugelmann,

Cut, lanced, etc., in short treated in every respect *secundum legem artis.** In spite of that the thing is continually breaking out again so that, with the exception of two or three days, I have been lying quite fallow for eight weeks. Last Saturday I went out again for the first time—Monday another relapse. I hope that it will finish this week, but who will guarantee me against new eruptions? It is extremely disagreeable. Moreover it attacks my head. My friend, Dr. Gumpert in Manchester, urges me to use arsenic. What do you think of it?

Your Koppel is not yet here.

Kertbeny is a German-Hungarian whose real name, between ourselves, is Benkert. The German-Hungarians love to Magyarise their names. I do not know him personally. Since he had a quarrel with Vogt about 1860, I asked him for some notes but received nothing of any use. (My Hungarian material was obtained partly from Szemere, partly from my own experience in London.) Later he applied to me in a quarrel he had with Kossuth. As far as I have been able to learn, there is nothing politically suspicious against him. He seems to be a literary busybody. His heresies with regard to Bonaparte are held by many otherwise honest eastern barbarians—in any case watch him. I also consider it more diplomatic not to show any mistrust of him (and for that reason I am enclosing the biographical notice which he requested). Nevertheless, as soon as the writing position no longer troubles me, I shall "order" information about him from other sources.

You guessed rightly about *Plagiarismus.*** I was intentionally uncivil and hair-raising in order to make Hofstetten suspect Liebknecht and to conceal my authorship. This between ourselves. You probably know that Engels and Siebel have got articles about my book published in the *Barmen-Zeitung, Elberfelder Zei-*

* According to all the rules of the art.
** The title of an anonymous article by Marx in the Berlin journal *Zukunft (Future)* of December 12, 1867, in which he proved that two Social-Democratic Reichstag deputies, Geib and Hofstetten, in their speeches used arguments from volume I of *Capital* without mentioning the author.

tung, Frankfurt Börsen-Zeitung and—to the great grief of Heinrich Bürgers—in the *Düsseldorf-Zeitung.* Siebel was the man in Barmen whose acquaintance I wanted you to make. He is now in Madeira for his health.

Last week the *Saturday Review*—the "blood and culture" paper —had a notice about my book in a review of recent German books. I have come off pretty well, as you will see from the following passage:

"The author's views may be as pernicious as we conceive them to be, but there can be no question as to the plausibility of his logic, the vigour of his rhetoric, and the charm with which he invests the driest problems of political economy."

Ouff!

My best greetings to your dear wife and Fränzchen. You will get other photographs from here, for we have now discovered that the water colours which looked good the first day dissolved in patches immediately after.

Write to me as often as your time permits. During my illness and the many occasions for vexation, letters from friends are very welcome.

Salut.

Yours,

K. M.

[Enclosed with this letter was the following autobiographical note for Kertbeny:]

Karl Marx, doctor of philosophy, born at Trier May 5, 1818.

1842-43. At first collaborator, then chief editor of the *Rheinische Zeitung* (Cologne). During the period that he edited the paper, it was subject to double censorship, a second censor being appointed by the government in addition to the local censor. Finally suppressed by order of the government. Marx left Germany and went to Paris. In 1844, in Paris, he published with A. Ruge the *Deutsch-Französischen Jahrbücher. (Franco-German Annuals).* In addition, *Die heilige Familie, Kritik der kritischen Kritik, gegen Bruno Bauer und Konsorten (The Holy Family, Critique of the Critical Criticism, contra Bruno Bauer and Company).*

December 1845, expelled from France by Guizot, at the instigation of the Prussian government, Marx went to Brussels, founded there, in 1846, the Association of German Workers, gave lectures on political economy, wrote for the *Réforme* (Paris), etc. . . .

1847: *Misère de la philosophie. Réponse à la Philosophie de la misère de M. Proudhon* (*The Poverty of Philosophy, Reply to M. Proudhon's Philosophy of Poverty*) ; ditto: *Discours sur le libre échange* (*Speech on Free Trade*) and various other pamphlets.

1848, in collaboration with F. Engels, *Manifesto of the Communist Party.* Arrested and expelled from Belgium, invited to France by a letter from the provisional government. Left France in April 1848, founded at Cologne the *Neue Rheinische Zeitung* (June 1848-May 1849). Marx was then expelled from Prussia, after the government had conducted an unsuccessful prosecution against him. Appeared twice in court (the first time to answer a charge against the paper, the second for inciting to rebellion; acquitted both times). Marx's speeches in his own defence were printed in *Two Political Processes* (Cologne).

1849. The last number—printed in red—of the *Neue Rheinische Zeitung.* Marx went to Paris. Expelled in September 1849 with the choice of being interned in Brittany (Morbihan). Refused and went to London where he is now living.

1850. Published the *Neue Rheinische Zeitung, politisch-okonomische Revue* (Hamburg).

1852. *The Eighteenth Brumaire of Louis Bonaparte* (New York). *Revelations Concerning the Communist Trial at Cologne.* This edition was confiscated at the German frontier, and a new edition was published in Boston in 1853.

1853-54. *Flysheets against Lord Palmerston.*

1859. *Contribution to the Critique of Political Economy* (Berlin).

1860. *Herr Vogt.*

1851-60. Regular contributor to the *New York Daily Tribune* and the *New American Cyclopædia.*

1861. Went to Berlin after the Amnesty; the Prussian government refused him renaturalisation.

1864. Published for the Central Council of the International Workingmen's Association the *Address to the Working Classes of Europe.*

1867. *Capital,* Vol. I (Hamburg).

London, March 6, 1868.

Dear Friend,

As soon as Koppel had gone, my health got worse again, although scarcely, I think, as a result of his departure. *Post, not propter.** (In any case he is in his own way quite a pleasant fellow. In my present state that particular way is too healthy to fit in very harmoniously with me.) That is the reason for my silence, so that I could not even acknowledge the receipt of Thünen. There is something touching about Thünen. A Mecklenburg *Junker* (true, with a *German* training in thinking) who treats his estate at Tellow as *the land* and Mecklenburg-Schwerin as *the town*, and who, proceeding from these premises, with the help of observation, the differential calculus, practical accounting, etc., constructs for himself the Ricardian theory of rent. It is at once worthy of respect and at the same time ridiculous.

I can now understand the curiously embarrassed tone of Herr Dühring's criticism. He is ordinarily a most bumptious, cheeky boy, who sets up as a revolutionary in political economy. He has done two things. He has published, firstly (proceeding from Carey) a *Critical Foundation of Political Economy* (about 500 pages) and, secondly, a new *Natural Dialectic* (against the Hegelian). My book has buried him from both sides. He gave it notice because of his hatred for Roscher, etc. For the rest, half intentionally, and half from lack of insight, he commits deceptions. He knows very well that my method of development is not Hegelian, since I am a materialist and Hegel is an idealist. Hegel's dialectic is the basic form of all dialectic, but only after it has been stripped of its mystical form, and it is precisely this which distinguishes my method. As for Ricardo, it really hurt Herr Dühring that in my treatment of Ricardo, the weak points in him, which Carey and a hundred others before him pointed out, do not even exist. Consequently he attempts, in *mauvaise foi*,** to burden me with all Ricardo's limitations. But never mind. I must be grateful to the man, since he is the first expert who has said anything at all.

In the second volume (which will certainly never appear if

* After, not because.
** Bad faith.

my health does not improve) property in land will be one of the subjects dealt with, competition only in so far as it is required for the treatment of the other themes.

During my illness (which I hope will soon cease altogether) I was unable to write, but I got down an enormous amount of "stuff," statistical and otherwise, which in itself would have been enough to make people sick who are not used to that sort of fodder and do not possess stomachs accustomed to digesting it rapidly.

My circumstances are very harassing, as I have been unable to do any additional work which would bring in money, and yet certain appearances must be maintained for the children's sake. If I did not have these two damned volumes to produce (and in addition to look for an English publisher) which can be done only in London, I would go to Geneva, where I could live very well with the means at my disposal. My daughter No. II is to marry at the end of this month.

Greetings to Fränzchen.

Yours,

K. M.

London, March 17, 1868.

Dear Friend,

Your letter affected me both unpleasantly and pleasantly (you see, I always move in dialectical contradictions).

Unpleasantly, because I know your circumstances and it would be rotten of me if I were to accept such presents at the *expense of your family*. I therefore regard these £15 as a loan, which I shall in time repay.

Pleasantly, not only as a mark of your great friendship (and in the bustle of the world friendship is the only personal thing that matters), but also because you have helped me out of a very difficult position in regard to the forthcoming marriage. Apart from medicines and doctors, I have spent so much money in the last four months on blue books, enquiries and Yankee reports, etc., on banks, that I really had nothing left for my daughter.

You may be sure that I have often discussed leaving London for Geneva, not only with myself and my family, but also with Engels. Here I have to spend from £400 to £500 annually; in Geneva I could live on £200. But *considered* all in all, it is for the time being *impossible*. I can finish my work only in London. And only *here* can I hope to draw at least a comparatively decent monetary profit from this work. But to do that I must *stay here* for a time. Apart from the fact that, if I were to leave here at this critical time, the whole labour movement, which I influence from behind the scenes, would fall into very bad hands and go the wrong way.

So, for the time being, all drawbacks notwithstanding, *fate* ties me to London. *Quant à* * Koppel, you do him wrong. Had I not been ill, he would have amused me and such a diversion never hurts the family.

Engels and I have not written for Liebknecht's paper hitherto. (Engels has now sent him two articles on my book.) Eccarius is the usual London correspondent.

Borkheim wrote an article against Herzen and company.

M.'s ** letter gave me great pleasure. But he has to some extent misunderstood my development of the subject. Otherwise he

*As to.
** Menke.

would have seen that I described *large-scale industry* not only as the mother of the antagonism, but also as the producer of the material and spiritual conditions for resolving that antagonism, although it is true the solution cannot proceed along pleasant lines.

With regard to Factory Acts—as the primary condition for giving the working class elbow room for development and movement—I demand them from the state, as a compulsory law, not only against the manufacturers, but against the workers themselves (on p. 542, note 52,* I refer to the resistance offered by working women to a limitation of the working day). If Herr M. develops the same energy as Owen, he can break that resistance. That the *individual manufacturer* (apart from the extent to which he tries to affect legislation) can do little in the matter, I also say on p. 243:** "But looking at things as a whole, all this does not, indeed, depend on the good or ill will of the individual capitalist," etc. See also note 114 [p. 260].*** That, nevertheless, the individual can do something has been clearly demonstrated by such manufacturers as Fielden, Owen, etc. Their main effectiveness must of course be of a public nature. As for the Dolfuses in Alsace, they are humbugs, who have managed, by the conditions enumerated in their contracts, to establish a comfortable serf-relationship to their workers which is at the same time very profitable to them. They have been thoroughly exposed in the Paris press and for that very reason one of the Dolfuses, a short time ago, introduced and got carried in the *corps législatif* **** one of the most infamous paragraphs of the press law—that *"la vie privée doit etre murée."* *****

With warmest greetings to your dear wife,

Yours,

KARL MARX.

À propos: Have you seen that my personal enemy, Schweitzer, has heaped eulogies on my head in six numbers of the *Sozialdemokrat* because of my book? Very painful for that old harlot Hatzfeld.

* P. 556, note 4, Eng. ed.
** P. 255, Eng. ed.
*** Note 2, p. 284, Eng. ed.
**** Legislative corps.
***** Private life should be enclosed by a wall.

London, April 6, 1868.

Dear Kugelmann,

The young pair were married at the registry office (since a church ceremony is not legally necessary here) and have left for France on their honeymoon. They send you and Frau Gertrude their best greetings.

Koppel called on me here. Unfortunately I could not receive him, as I was wrapped up in plasters. Engels came here for the wedding and left again yesterday. On his advice I have decided to take the arsenic cure, since this state of things must after all be brought to an end. One of his friends in Manchester was completely cured in a relatively short time by using arsenic. I had certain prejudices against it after reading in the *Medical Journal* the report of a discussion held by French doctors.

The Irish question is dominant here just now. Of course, it has been exploited by Gladstone and company only in order to get into office again, and to have, above all, an *electoral cry* at the next elections, which will be based on household suffrage. For the moment this turn in affairs is bad for the workers' party; the intriguers among the workers, such as Odger and Potter, who want to get into the next parliament, have now a new excuse for joining up with the bourgeois liberals.

However, this is only a *penalty* which England—and consequently the English working class—is paying for its terrible century-long crime against Ireland. And in the long run it will be good for the English working class itself. You see, the English established church in Ireland—or what they used to call here the Irish church—is the religious bulwark of *English landlordism in Ireland,* and at the same time the outpost of the established church in England itself. (I am speaking here of the established church as a landowner.) The overthrow of the established church in Ireland will mean its downfall in England and the two will be followed (in decline) by landlordism—first in Ireland and then in England. I have, however, been convinced from the first that the social revolution must begin *seriously* from the bottom, that is, from landed proprietorship.

Apart from that, it will have this very useful result: that, once the Irish church is dead, the Protestant Irish tenants in the prov-

5*

ince of Ulster will unite with the Catholic tenants in the three other provinces of Ireland and join their movement; whereas up to the present landlordism has been able to exploit this religious hostility.

The day before yesterday I received a letter from Freiligrath (wedding cards * were of course sent to him) in which the following curious sentence occurs. But it will perhaps amuse you more if I enclose the letter itself, which I now do. But you must send it back to me. Just the following, so that you may understand the letter properly: Shortly before my book appeared, *Zwölf Streiter der Revolution,** * by G. Struve and Gustav Rasch, was published in Berlin. In this memorial Freiligrath is acclaimed as "one" of the twelve apostles, and at the same time it is demonstrated to a nicety that he *never* was a communist and in fact only came to be associated with such monsters as Marx, Engels, Wolff, etc., by too great a condescension. Since Wolff was also attacked, I wrote to Freiligrath for an explanation, the more so as I knew that G. Rasch (a scoundrel) was at the head of his begging committee in Berlin.*** He answered me very drily and with evasive philistine cunning. Later I sent him my book, without, however, as was formerly our mutual custom, inscribing my name. He seems to have taken the hint.

Best regards to your dear wife and Fränzchen. If it is at all possible I shall come in any circumstances and pay you a visit.

Yours,
K. MARX.

À propos: Borkheim will visit you in few days.—Do not forget that in spite of all comradeship with him, I always maintain a certain reserve.

Liebknecht's paper is too narrow-mindedly "southern. . . ." [The last line is undecipherable; the photocopy is damaged.]

* The marriage of Marx's second daughter, Laura, to Paul Lafargue took place at the end of April.
** *Twelve Fighters of the Revolution.*
*** In 1867 collections were made for a national gift to Freiligrath, following the crash of a Swiss bank of which he was the London representative.

[The enclosed letter from Freiligrath is as follows:]
II Portland Place, Lower Clapton, N.E.

April 3, 1868.

Dear Marx,

The receipt of Laura's wedding card today gave us the most pleasant surprise. We had no idea that the great event was so near and now send the young pair, as well as you and your dear wife, our best wishes from the bottom of our hearts.

And now let me at last thank you for the friendly remembrance you showed in sending me the first volume of your *Kapital* and do not, because it comes so late, think my gratitude the less warm or sincere. I had intended all the time to thank you personally, but in all the work and excitement that the last few months have brought me I could not find the time. So let me thank you now and be assured that, if anybody is, certainly I am one of the many who rejoice in recognising and admiring the spirit, the knowledge and the amazing diligence with which you have, in this work, built yourself a *monomentum aere perennius.**

You know I am not an expert (merely an economist "in sentiment") and will not therefore demand of me a detailed judgment—but I can say that from reading, or rather from studying your book, I have already drawn the most varied instruction and the most abundant enjoyment.

It is really a book that should be studied and therefore its success will not, perhaps, be very rapid or loud; but it will quietly produce an effect that will be all the more profound and lasting. I know that in the Rhineland many young merchants and factory owners are enthusiastic about the book. In these circles it will accomplish its real purpose—and will in addition be an indispensable source of reference for the man of learning. Again my warmest thanks. And at the next opportunity you will also write your name in my copy, won't you?

Our Louise is also engaged to be married. Once the infantile sickness of engagement and marriage-making seizes hold of a house, nothing can stop it. It must take its course. The matrimonial measles!

But the marriage is still a long way off. Louise is still very young and must wait. Her fiancé is Heinrich Wiens, a cousin of Kätchen's husband and also a regular Baltic pirate, like those who captured the daughters of the old poets.

I hope your health is better again. We shall soon come over and convince ourselves about it. Meanwhile the most cordial greetings to you and your ladies from us all.

Yours,
F. FREILIGRATH.

* A monument more lasting than bronze.

London, April 17, 1868.

Dear Kugelmann,

You must think me a great criminal for sending such a belated reply to your dear wife and to your own kind letter. The fact is simply this: the old bloodroses (to express myself poetically) have attacked me with such tactical cunning, that I cannot put myself in the position necessary for writing. It is true I could have dictated a letter. But you know in such cases one is always hoping to be all right again the following day. Hence the delay. Hence also these few lines.

I do not know when I shall be able to come to Germany for a few days; in any case it will not be soon. However, I shall come at a time when I know that you will not be away.

You have done me a great service by writing to Virchov, although I doubt whether he has the time and patience to go deeply into a subject so remote from his own. I know that I had to exercise the greatest self-control to read his *Cellular Pathology* in Manchester, particularly because of his style.

The issues of the *Sozialdemokrat* concerned with my book are: No. 10 (22 January, 1868), No. 11 (24 January), No. 12 (26 January), No. 14 (31 January), No. 15 (2 February), No. 24 (23 February), No. 25 (26 February), No. 30 (8 March) and another number, which I have not got at the moment, but which only contained extracts.

With cordial greetings to your dear wife and Fränzchen.

Yours,

K. Marx.

Meyer visited me here.

London, June 24, 1868.

Dear Friend,

I was prevented by all sorts of incidents from writing to you. Even now only a few lines.

My eldest and youngest daughters have both got scarlatina. I remember that in Hanover you spoke to me of the treatment required once the crisis was passed and the scaling-off process begins. Will you be so kind as to write me about it at once.

With best greetings to your dear wife and Fränzchen.

Yours,

K. Marx.

Liebknecht is growing more and more imbecile in his South-German stupidity. He is not enough of a dialectician to criticise both sides at the same time.

London, July 2, 1868.

Dear Kugelmann,

Best thanks for your letter. The children are getting on well, although they are not yet well enough to go out (today is the ninth day).

As for my book, I received five copies of the *Elberfelder-Zeitung* yesterday, containing a very benevolent review by Dr. Schnake (I know the name from 1848, but do not know him personally).* There is a good deal of confusion in his presentation of the matter. On the other hand, I am informed from Berlin that clown Faucher makes merry over my book in the June number of his journal.** It is good that the gentlemen at last give vent to their annoyance.

I do not yet know if and when I am coming to Germany. I am at last free of carbuncles.

Engels is certainly going over in August or September.

Salut! And my compliments to Mrs. Kugelmann and the little one.

Yours,

K. MARX.

---

* This refers to an article by Friedrich Schnake who in the 'forties was a prominent representative of German "true socialism" and contributed to papers of this tendency in the Rhine district.
** *Vierteljahrschrift für Volkswirtschaft und Kulturgeschichte (Quarterly Review of National Economy and the History of Culture).*

London, July 11, 1868.

Dear Friend,

The children are getting on well, although still weak.

Thank you very much for the things you sent. Do *not* write to Faucher, otherwise that *mannequin piss* * will think himself too important. All that he has achieved is to induce me, when a second edition comes out, to make a few necessary thrusts at Bastiat in the part about the *magnitude of value*. This was not done before because the third volume will contain a separate and detailed chapter about the "vulgar economy" gentlemen. You will find it quite natural for Faucher and company to deduce the "exchange value" of their scribbling not from the *quantity of labour power expended*, but from the *absence of such expenditure*, that is, from *"saved labour."* And the worthy Bastiat did not even himself make this "discovery," so welcome to those gentlemen, but as was his custom, just "copied" many earlier authors. The sources used are of course unknown to Faucher and company.

As for the *Zentralblatt*, the man is making the greatest possible concession in admitting that, if one means anything at all by value, the conclusions I draw must be accepted. The unfortunate fellow does not see that, even if there were no chapter on "value" in my book, the analysis of the real relationships which I give would contain the proof and demonstration of the real value relation. The nonsense about the necessity of proving the concept of value arises from complete ignorance both of the subject dealt with and of the method of science. Every child knows that a country which ceased to work, I will not say for a year, but for a few weeks, would die. Every child knows, too, that the mass of products corresponding to the different needs require different and quantitatively determined masses of the total labour of society. That this necessity of distributing social labour in definite proportions cannot be done away with by the *particular form* of social production, but can only change the *form it assumes*, is self evident. No natural laws can be done away with. What can change, in changing historical circumstances, is the *form* in which these laws operate. And the form in which this propor-

* The well-known fountain-figure in Brussels.

tional division of labour operates, in a state of society where the interconnection of social labour is manifested in the *private exchange* of the individual products of labour, is precisely the *exchange value* of these products.

The science consists precisely in working out *how* the law of value operates. So that if one wanted at the very beginning to "explain" all the phenomena which apparently contradict that law, one would have to give the science *before* the science. It is precisely Ricardo's mistake that in his first chapter on value he takes as given all possible categories, which have still to be developed, in order to prove their conformity with the law of value.

On the other hand as you correctly assumed, *the history of the theory* certainly shows that the concept of the value relation has *always been the same*, whether more or less clear, hedged with illusions or scientifically precise. Since the thought process itself grows out of the conditions, is itself a *natural process*, thinking that really comprehends must always be the same, and can only vary gradually according to maturity of development, including that of the organ by which the thinking is done. Everything else is drivel.

The vulgar economist has not the faintest idea that the actual everyday exchange relations need not be directly identical with the magnitudes of value. The point of bourgeois society consists precisely in this, that *a priori* there is no conscious social regulation of production. The reasonable and the necessary in nature asserts itself only as a blindly working average. And then the vulgar economist thinks he has made a great discovery, when, as against the disclosures of the inner connection, he proudly claims that in appearance things look different.

In fact, he is boasting that he holds fast to the appearance, and takes it for the last word. Why, then, any science at all?

But the matter has also another background. When the inner connection is grasped, all theoretical belief in the permanent necessity of existing conditions breaks down before their practical collapse. Here, therefore, it is in the interest of the ruling classes to perpetuate this unthinking confusion. And for what other purpose are the sycophantic babblers paid, who have no other scientific trump to play, save that in political economy one should not think at all?

But *satis supraque*.* In any case it shows what these priests of the bourgeoisie have come to, when workers and even manufacturers and merchants understand my book and find their way about in it, while these "scribes" (!) complain that I make excessive demands on their understanding.

I would not advise the reprint of Schweitzer's article, although Schweitzer has made a good job of it for his paper.

You will oblige me by sending a few copies of the *Staatsanzeiger*.

You will get Schnake's address on enquiry at the *Elberfelder*.

Best greetings to your wife and Fränzchen.

Yours,

K. M.

À propos: I have received an article from Dietzgen about my book; I am sending it to Liebknecht.

---

* Enough and more than enough.

London, August 10, 1868.

Dear Kugelmann,

On receiving your letter I did what I could, but in vain. At the moment it is impossible to get money for foreign strikes from the unions here. I find the variety of information about the Lindon factory contained in the Hanoverian papers finally sent to me very interesting.

My family is at present at the seaside which was the more necessary as both the girls were very weak after their illness. Lafargue, after having passed his surgery examinations here in London, will perform operations in a hospital as assistant surgeon for a few weeks and then move to Paris, where he still has to take the French medical examinations.

At the moment I am more concerned with private than with public economy. Engels has offered to guarantee a loan of £100-£150 for me at 5 per cent interest, the first half to be paid in January, the second in July. Up to the present, however, I have not been able to find the lender.

I hope very much that the *state of my work* will permit me to leave London for good and go to the Continent next year, at the end of September. I shall break away as soon as I can dispense with the Museum here. The dearness of living here is becoming more and more burdensome as time goes on. It is true that the pettiness of conditions over there is not much to my taste. However, *"Ruhe ist die erste Bürgerpflicht"* * and it is the only way of attaining peace. There are all sorts of scandals here concerning the so-called French branch of the International Workingmen's Association, about which I shall report in my next letter.

I am now *solus* ** and it seems strange to be without all the noise of the children.

Salut.

Yours,

K. MARX.

* "To keep the peace is the first duty of the citizen." From a proclamation posted in Berlin, October 17, 1806, after the battle of Jena, which began with the words "The King has lost a battle," and continued as above.
** Alone.

London, October 12, 1868.

My dear Friend,

Your obstinate silence is quite incomprehensible to me. Did I give cause for it in some way in my last letter? I hope not. In any case it was unintentional. I need not tell you explicitly, you *know*, that you are my most intimate friend in Germany and I do not see that, *inter amicos,** it is necessary to keep such a sharp watch on one another for any trifle. Least of all have you *this* *right* in regard to me, because you know how much I am obliged to you. You have done more—apart from everything personal— for my book than all Germany put together. But, perhaps, you are so energetically silent in order to show me that you are not like the crowd of so-called friends who are silent when things go badly and speak when they go well. But there was no need for such a "demonstration" on your part. When I speak of a "good state of affairs" I mean, firstly, the propaganda which my book has been doing and the recognition which it has found among the German workers, since you wrote me last. And, secondly, there is the wonderful progress which the International Work- ingmen's Association has made, especially in England.

A few days ago a Petersburg publisher surprised me with the news that a Russian translation of *Das Kapital* is now being printed. He asked for my photograph for the title page and I could not deny this trifle to "my good friends," the Russians. It is an irony of fate that the Russians, whom I have fought for twenty-five years, and not only in German, but in French and English, have always been my "patrons." In Paris in 1843 and 1844 the Russian aristocrats there treated me most tenderly. My book against Proudhon (1847) and the one published by Duncker (1859) have had a greater sale in Russia than any- where else. And the first foreign nation to translate *Kapital* is the Russian. But too much should not be made of all this. The Russian aristocracy is, in its youth, educated at German univer- sities and in Paris. They always run after the most extreme that the West can offer.

It is pure *gourmandise,*** such as a part of the French aris- tocracy practised during the eighteenth century. *Ce n'est pas pour*

---

* Among friends.
** Fine feeding.

*les tailleurs et les bottiers,** Voltaire said of his own enlightenment. This does not prevent the same Russians, once they enter State service, from becoming rascals.

I am having a good deal of bother just now in Germany in connection with the quarrels of the leaders, as you can see from the enclosed letters, which you will please return. On the one side, Schweitzer, who has nominated me Pope *in partibus infidelium,*** so that I can proclaim him the "workers' emperor" of Germany. On the other side, Liebknecht, who forgets that Schweitzer, in point of fact, forced him to remember that there is a proletarian movement apart from the petty-bourgeois democratic movement.

I hope that you and your family are well. And I hope that I have not fallen into disfavour with your dear wife. *À propos*: the International Women's Association, *duce* Frau Gögg (read Geck),*** has sent an epistle to the Brussels Congress, enquiring whether ladies may join. The answer, of course, was a courteous affirmative. Should you therefore persist in your silence, I shall send your wife a mandate as correspondent of the General Council.

I have suffered a good deal from the heat, because of my liver, but am at the moment well.

Salut.

Yours,

KARL MARX.

P. S. 1. The Spanish revolution came like a *deus ex machina**** to prevent the otherwise inevitable and disastrous Franco-Prussian war.

P. S. 2. You wrote me once that I am to receive a book by Büchner. When and how?

---

* This is not for tailors and cobblers.
** In the country of the infidels, *i.e.*, a functionary without a function.
*** Geck in German=fop.
**** God out of the machine. A favourite device of the ancient Greek dramatists whereby a god suddenly makes his appearance on the scene out of some theatrical machinery and provides a happy solution of the apparently hopelessly entangled situation.

London, October 26, 1868.

My dear Friend,

Since at this moment, when your letter arrives, I am plagued with a visit, I shall write just these few lines.

Kertbeny's address: No. I/III (what the III means I do not know; perhaps, third floor) Behrenstrasse.

Now permit me a word. Since you and Engels were of the opinion that it would be useful, I gave way to having this advertisement in the *Gartenlaube*. I was *decisively opposed to it*. And now I ask you *urgently, to give up* this joke *definitely*. It leads to nothing except that fellows like Keil and "Daheim" believe that one belongs to the pack of great literary and other men, and needs or desires their protection.

I think it is more harmful than useful and beneath the dignity of a scientific man. For example, Meyer's *Konversationslexikon* wrote asking me for a biography a long time ago. Not only did I not send one, but I did not even answer their letter. Everybody must reach salvation in his own way. As for Kertbeny, he is a confused, boastful, importunate literary idler and the less one has to do with him, the better.

Salut.

Yours,

K. M.

London, December 5, 1868.

Dear Kugelmann,

Have you got Dietzgen's address? A fairly long time ago he sent me a fragment of a manuscript on the "faculty of thought" which, in spite of a certain confusion and of too frequent repetition, contains much that is excellent and—as the independent product of a working man—admirable. I did not answer immediately after reading it, because I wanted to hear what Engels thought of it; so I sent him the manuscript. It was a long time before I got it back. And now I *cannot find* Dietzgen's letter, with his new address. You see, he wrote me in his last letter from Petersburg that he was returning to the Rhine and would establish himself there. Have you received his new address? If so, please send it to me by return. My conscience—one never quite gets rid of that sort of thing—is troubling me for having left Dietzgen so long without a reply. You also promised to tell me something about him personally.

I have received Büchner's Lectures on Darwinism. He is obviously a "maker of books" and probably that is why he is called "Büchner," the superficial nonsense about the history of materialism is obviously copied from Lange. The way in which such a pigmy disposes, for example, of Aristotle—a materialist of quite a different brand from Büchner—is truly astonishing. He is very naive, too, when he says of Cabanis: "One almost thinks one is listening to Karl Vogt." Probably Cabanis has copied Vogt!

I promised some time ago to write to you about the French branch. These ragamuffins are, half or three-quarters of them, *maquereaux,** and such like rabble; but all of them—since our people have withdrawn—are heroes of the revolutionary world, who, from a safe distance of course, kill kings and emperors, but especially Louis Napoleon. In their eyes we are naturally reactionaries, and they drew up against us, with all due formality, an indictment which was in fact submitted to the Brussels Congress **—in the closed sessions. The anger of these blacklegs was increased when Felix Pyat, a shipwrecked fourth-rate French

* Procurers.
** The Brussels Congress of the First International held in September 1868.

author of melodrama, who in the Revolution of '48 was only used as a toastmaster (that is what the English call the men *paid* to give the toasts at public dinners, or to direct the order of the toasts) and who has a perfect monomania for "shouting in a whisper" and playing the dangerous conspirator, had got them under his control. Pyat wanted to use this gang to make the International Workingmen's Association a tool of his. He was particularly anxious to compromise us. At a public meeting which the French branch proclaimed and trumpeted in large placards as a meeting of the "International Association," Louis Napoleon, alias Badinguest, was *solemnly condemned to death*, the execution of the sentence, of course, being left to the nameless Brutuses of Paris. Since the English press took no notice of this farce, we too have been content to pass it over in silence. But one of the gang—a certain Vesinier, a blackmailing journalist— broadcast the whole wretched affair through a Belgian paper, *La Cigale*, which claims to be an organ of the International, a sort of "comic" paper, the like of which exists nowhere else in Europe. You see, there is nothing comic in it except its gravity. From *La Cigale* the thing found its way into *Le Pays, Journal de l'Empire*. It was of course an unexpected feast for Paul de Cassagnac. Thereupon we—that is, the General Council—declared officially in six lines in the *Cigale*, that F. Pyat had no connection *whatever* with the International, of which he was not even a member. *Hinc illae irea.** This war of the frogs and mice ended in the French branch withdrawing with a roar and carrying on business on its own account, under Pyat's ægis. They have founded here in London, as an auxiliary, a so-called German Agitation League, about eighteen strong, with an old Pfalz refugee, the half crazy watchmaker Weber, at the head. Now you know everything that there is to report about this solemn, high-sounding and important event. But one thing more. We had the satisfaction of seeing that Blanqui got one of his friends to ridicule Pyat, also in the *Cigale*, leaving him the alternative of being recognised either as a monomaniac or a police agent.

Yesterday evening I got a letter from Schweitzer in which he

* Hence this anger.

lets me know that he is again going to prison and that the outbreak of a civil war—that is, war between him and W. Liebknecht—is inevitable. I must say that Schweitzer is right on one point, that is, Liebknecht's incapacity. His paper is really pitiful. How a man whom I crammed orally for fifteen years (he was always too lazy to read) can print such rubbish as for example *Society and the State*, in which "the social" (another fine category!) is treated as "the secondary" and the "political" as the essential would be incomprehensible, if Liebknecht were not a South German and, as it seems, had always mistaken me for his old superior, the "noble" Gustav Struve.

Lafargue and wife have now been in Paris two months. The authorities in Paris do not want to recognise the medical honours which he won in London, and require him to pass five new "Parisian" examinations.

From next year, my economic (not political-economic) circumstances will be adequate for my needs as the result of a settlement.

With best greetings to your dear wife and Fränzchen.

Yours,

K. MARX.

Is your wife also active in the great German campaign for the emancipation of women? I think the German women should have begun by driving their men to self-emancipation.

London, December 12, 1868.

Dear Friend,

I wanted to write you in more detail, but am prevented from doing so by unforeseen foreign "affairs." Do not let that prevent you from taking up the pen again soon.

The letter from Freund (enclosed with my thanks) interested me greatly. It is high time for others to appear on the scene in Germany besides the present "standard-bearers" of science.

I am also returning Dietzgen's portrait. The story of his life is not quite what I had imagined it to be, although I always had a feeling that he was "not a worker like Eccarius." It is true that the sort of philosophic outlook which he has worked out for himself requires a certain amount of peace and leisure which the everyday workman does not enjoy. I have got two very good workmen living in New York, A. Vogt, a shoe-maker, and Siegfried Meyer, a mining engineer, both from Berlin. A third workman who could give lectures on my book is Lochner, a carpenter (common working man), who has been here in London about 15 years.

Tell your wife I never "suspected" her of being one of generaless Geck's subordinates. My question was only intended as a joke. In any case ladies cannot complain of the *International*, for it has elected a lady, Madame Law, to be a member of the General Council.

Joking aside, great progress was evident in the last Congress of the American "Labour Union" in that, among other things, it treated working women with complete equality. While in this respect the English, and still more the gallant French, are burdened with a spirit of narrow-mindedness. Anybody who knows anything of history knows that great social changes are impossible without the feminine ferment. Social progress can be measured exactly by the social position of the fair sex (the ugly ones included).

About the "settlement": from the outset there could not be any question of my taking up business before my book is ready. Otherwise I could long ago have extricated myself from any painful situation.

The fact is simply this—but *entirely between ourselves*—that.

6*

on the one hand, I came to an arrangement with my family; on the other hand, Engels, without my knowledge, came to an agreement with his partner about his own income (since he is retiring from the business in June) as a result of which a settlement was made which will enable me, from next year, to work in peace.

With best greetings,

Yours,

K. M.

London, February 11, 1869.

Dear Friend,

The delay in this letter is due to two circumstances. Firstly, the damned foggy weather here—nothing but mist—gave me an extraordinarily severe *grippe*, which lasted nearly four weeks. Secondly, the enclosed photographs were taken at least seven weeks ago, but only just recently could copies be made from the plate, because of the same weather and the atmospheric darkness.

The enclosed letter from A. Ruge was given to my friend Strohn in Bradford by one of his business friends. Ruge obviously could not resist the "negation of negation." You must send the letter back to me at once, because Strohn has to return it to the addressee.

The treasurer of our General Council, Cowell Stepney—a very rich and distinguished man, but wholly, if in somewhat foolish fashion, devoted to the workers' cause—enquired of a friend in Bonn about literature (German) dealing with the labour question and socialism. The friend sent him *en réponse* * a list made out by Dr. Held, Professor of Political Economy at Bonn. His comments show the terrible limitations of these learned mandarins. He (Held) writes about me and Engels:

"*Engels—The Condition of the Working Class in England*, etc. The best product of German socialist-communist literature. Closely connected with Engels is Karl Marx, the author of the most scientific and most erudite work which Socialism as a whole can boast of, *Das Kapital*. Although it has only recently appeared, this book is still an echo (!) of the movement of 1848. That is why I mention it here in connection with Engels. The work is at the same time (!) of great interest for the present because (!!) in it we may study the source of Lassalle's basic ideas." Fine company to be in!

A reader in political economy at a German university writes me that I have quite convinced him, but—but his position compels him, "like other colleagues," *not to express* his convictions.

This cowardice of the experts, on the one side, and the conspiracy of silence of the bourgeois and reactionary press, on the

* In reply.

other, is doing me great harm. Meissner writes that the accounts for the autumn quarter turned out badly. He is still 200 thalers below the cost of production. He adds: "If in a few large places such as Berlin, etc., half as much had been done, as Kugelmann has done in Hanover, we should already have had a second edition."

I became a grandfather on the 1st of January; the new year present was a little boy. Lafargue has at last managed to get excused from three examinations and now has only two to take in France.

With best greetings to your dear wife and Fränzchen.

Yours,

KARL MARX.

The cross which my eldest daughter, Jenny, is wearing in the photograph is a Polish insurrection cross of 1864.

[The text of the letter from Ruge mentioned above is as follows:]

7 Park Crescent,
January 25, 1869,
Brighton.

Dear Mr. Steinthal,

Simultaneously with this letter I am having sent to you by book post Marx on *Capital*.

Most cordial thanks! This book has kept me continuously occupied all the time, although I have had to work at all sorts of subsidiary things as well.

It is an *epoch-making book* and sheds a brilliant, often piercing light on the development, decline and the birth pangs and frightfully painful days of social periods.

The proof of *surplus value* through unpaid labour, of the expropriation of the workers who worked on their own account and of the approaching expropriation of expropriators, are classical.

The last on page 745 *: "The capitalist mode of appropriation, the result of the capitalist mode of production, produces capitalist private property. This is the first negation of individual private property, as founded on the labour of the proprietor. But capitalist production begets, with the inexorability of a law of Nature, its own negation. It is the negation of negation. This does not re-establish private property for the producer, but gives him individual property based on the acquisitions of the capitalist era: i.e., on cooperation and the possession in common of the land and of the means of production."

Marx possesses a wide erudition and a magnificent dialectical talent.

* English edition, page 789.

The book exceeds the horizon of many men and newspaper writers; but it will quite certainly make its way through and in spite of the broad foundation, indeed, just because of it, it will exercise a powerful influence.

With reference to religion, the author very pertinently remarks on page 608 *: "As, in religion, man is governed by the products of his own brain, so in capitalist production he is governed by the products of his own hand."

And in order to set him free, it is far from sufficient to throw a light in the eyes of the owl; indeed, if he ever loses his master, like the Frenchman or the Spaniard, he himself sets him up again over himself.

Anyhow, much happiness for the year 1869! May it prove itself like its predecessors! My best greetings to Frau Steinthal and Herr Heydemann!

Entirely yours,

Dr. A. Ruge.

* English edition, page 635.

London, March 3, 1869.

Dear Kugelmann,

The damned photographer has again been leading me by the nose for several weeks and has not yet supplied additional prints. But I shall not on that account put off this letter any longer.

As regards *Herr Vogt*, I wanted to get the copies that could still be rescued from Liebknecht into a safe place (I had sent him 300 copies from London to Berlin, that is, all the copies then left) in case they should be needed. I therefore took the liberty of having them sent on to you.

Aber, Oerindur, lös mir dieses Räzsel der Natur!" * Liebknecht sent you six whole copies, yet informed me that he sent you fifty. Will you please ask him to unravel the mystery?

Quételét is now too old to start any new experiments with him. In the past he rendered a great service by demonstrating how even the apparent accidents of social life possess, in their periodic recurrence and their periodic averages, an inner necessity. But he never attained to the interpretation of this necessity. He has actually made no progress, but has only extended the material of his observations and calculations. He is no further today than he was *before* 1830.

It will certainly be well into summer before I have the second volume ready. Then—I and my daughter will come to Germany with the manuscript, and will see you then. Or rather visit you.

A very interesting movement is going on in France. The Parisians are making a regular study of their recent revolutionary past, in order to prepare themselves for the business of the impending new revolution. First the *origin of the Empire*—then the *coup d'état of December.* This had been completely forgotten, just as the reaction in Germany succeeded in stamping out the memory of 1848-49.

That is why Tènot's books on the *coup d'état* attracted such enormous attention in Paris and the provinces that in a short time they went through ten impressions. They were followed by dozens of other books on the same period. *C'était la rage* **

* "But, Oerindur, solve for me this riddle of Nature." A line occurring in a German play, *Die Schuld* (*The Guilt*), by Müllner, the hero of which was a Count Oerindur.
** It was all the rage.

and therefore soon became a speculative business for the publishers.

These books were written by the opposition—Tènot, for example, is one of the *Siècle* * men (I mean the liberal bourgeois paper, not our "century"). All the liberal scoundrels and illiberal scoundrels who belong to the official opposition patronise this *mouvement*.** Also the republican democrats, people like, for example, Delescluze, formerly Ledru Rollin's adjutant, and now, as a republican patriarch, editor of the Paris *Réveil*.

Up to the present everybody has been revelling in these posthumous disclosures or rather reminiscences, everybody who is not Bonapartist.

But then came the other side of the medal. First of all the French government itself got the renegade Hippolyte Castille to publish *Les Massacres de Juin, 1848*. This was a blow for Thiers, Falloux, Marie, Jules Favre, Jules Simon, Pelletan, etc., in short, for the chiefs of what is called in France *l'Union Liberale*,*** who want to get away with the next elections, the infamous old dogs!

Then, however, came the Socialist Party, which "exposed" the opposition—and the republican democrats of the old style. Among others, Vermorel: *Les Hommes de 1848* **** and *L'Opposition*.

Vermorel is a Proudhonist.

Last came the Blanquists, for example, G. Tridon: *Gironde et Girondins*.

And so the whole historic witches' cauldron is bubbling.

When shall *we* be so far!

To show you how well the French police are served: I intended to go to Paris early next week to see my daughter.

Last Saturday a police agent enquired at Lafargue's whether Monsieur Marx had already arrived. He had a commission for him. Forewarned!

My most cordial greetings to your dear wife and Fränzchen. How is Madame Tenge?

Yours,
K. M.

* Century.
** Movement.
*** This was an alliance of all the liberal parties in opposition to Napoleon III.
**** *The Men of 1848*.

London, May 11, 1869.

Dear Kugelmann,

You must forgive my protracted silence. Firstly I have for several weeks been suffering from my liver complaint, which always afflicts me in the spring months and is the more troublesome in that it makes me almost entirely unfit for intellectual work. Secondly, however, I have been waiting from one day to the next for the photograph that you want and that Herr Fahnenbach, a German sleepyhead, has not delivered to this day.

My wife and youngest daughter are at the moment visiting the Lafargues in Paris, so that we are very lonely here.

With the best will in the world, I could not find any Palmerston pamphlets (mine) for you. The Urquhart publications against Russia and Palmerston, although containing a good deal that is correct, spoil everything through the crotchets of the great "David."

Your article sent to Engels. It will be difficult for us, in our complete isolation from the respectable press, to do anything for you in this field, but we shall try.

About the end of August I intend visiting you with my daughter and spending till the end of September with you in Germany, wherever you like, even at the risk of neglecting to finish my manuscript. I cannot, of course, stay any longer than that.

I read your letter to Borkheim. You say quite rightly that the St. Bartholomew nonsense about the Belgian massacres will not do. But you in your turn overlook the importance and the peculiar meaning of these events. Belgium, you must know, is the only country, where, year in, year out, swords and muskets have the last word to say in strikes. In an address of the General Council here, which I wrote in English and French, the situation is made clear. By tomorrow the English address will be ready. I will send it to you immediately.

I have also just written an English address for the General Council of the International Association to the National Labour Union in the United States, in reference to the war with England, which the bourgeois republicans are just now wanting to stage.

Herr Meissner has had the (printed and corrected) manuscript of the *18. Brumaire* since the end of January, but has constantly delayed printing it. That's pleasant too! He waits until the time when it would be effective is past, from stupid booksellers' business reasons.

With best greetings to your dear wife and Fränzchen.

Yours,

KARL MARX.

London, July 15, 1869.

Dear Kugelmann,

Your letter of 2 June came while I was in Manchester. They forgot to send it on to me and later forgot its existence completely. I have *only just* found it, my attention having been called to it by your letter of 6 July. I only got this second letter yesterday because, as my Laura was ill, I have spent eight days *incognito* in Paris where, by the by, the growing movement is palpable. Otherwise I should have hastened to write to you while you were ill.

As for the *18. Brumaire,* Meissner's assurances are sheer evasions. He has had the thing since the end of January. Naturally, he did not get the preface, because he had not sent the last two proof-sheets. I got those at last on 23 June and sent them back corrected the same day, together with the preface. So more than three weeks have passed again, until we are really landed in the dull season of the book trade.

I shall not come to Germany till September. I shall make the journey mainly because of my daughter. But in any case I would come to visit you in Heligoland (I am travelling through Hanover).

As to the biography by Engels, please send it back to me. He must rewrite it, as it is intended for a different public.

With cordial greetings to your dear wife and Fränzchen.

Yours,

K. M.

London, July 30, 1869.

Dear Friend,

I had an abscess (carbunculous) for about 12 days (not yet quite healed) on my left arm, like the one that I had under the left armpit while I was staying with Engels in Manchester. But that is not the reason why I have delayed until today my answer to your letter of 17. inst.

Since I would be most unwilling to cut across your plans, and was also personally interested in enjoying your company, I tried several ways of arranging the affair to fit in with your intentions. But it is *absolutely impossible*. At the end of August I *must* be in Holland with my relatives, where I have many affairs to settle that are of great interest and importance to me. My suggestion, to postpone the rendezvous to another time, was emphatically turned down because the people I am to meet are all tied to their business and can only meet me in Brussels at that particular time.

So I shall leave London about the end of August. You must let me know when you will be back in Hanover. I shall see how far I can regulate my further progress to fit in.

With best greetings to your dear wife and Fränzchen.

Yours,

K. M.

London, October 12, 1869.

Dear Kugelmann,

In all haste, as Tussychen * and Engels have just arrived. You see from these lines that we arrived safely in England, yesterday.

We had a few sea adventures, and others, about which Jennychen will write you.

Meanwhile, our heartiest greetings to the whole house.

Yours,

K. M.

Special greetings to Madame la Comtesse and Käuzchen. Ditto greetings from Engels, Lafargue, Mrs. Marx, etc. The little one is better again.

* Eleanor Marx.

London, November 29, 1869.

Dear Kugelmann,

About five weeks ago Jennychen sent you a letter—in fact two letters, one to you and one to the Countess. In that letter there was a portrait of G. Weerth—and since it is difficult to replace, and there is not a second one that could be sent, Jennychen would like to know as soon as possible whether you received it or not.

Some suspicion as to the inviolability and safety of the Post has been aroused here because a letter, which I wrote to Engels from Hanover, was unmistakably forced open and very clumsily sealed up again. Engels had saved the envelope, that I might convince myself by ocular inspection.

You must explain my long and to a certain extent criminal silence by the amount of work which I had to make up, not only in my scientific studies, but also *quoad* * the *International;* by my having to study *Russian,* because of a book sent to me from Petersburg about the condition of the working class (peasants, of course, included) in Russia, and, finally, by the anything but satisfactory state of my health.

You will probably have seen in the *Volksstaat* the resolutions against Gladstone, which I proposed, on the question of the Irish amnesty. I have now attacked Gladstone—and it has attracted attention here—just as I formerly attacked Palmerston. The demagogic refugees here love to fall upon the Continental despots from a safe distance. That sort of thing only attracts me, when it happens *vultu instantis tyranni.***

Nevertheless, both my utterance on this Irish amnesty question and my further proposal to the General Council, to discuss the relation of the English working class to Ireland and to pass resolutions on it have of course other objects besides that of speaking out loudly and decidedly for the oppressed Irish against their oppressors.

I have become more and more convinced—and the only question is to bring this conviction home to the English working class—that it can never do anything decisive here in England

* In regard to.
** In the face of the tyrant.

until it separates its policy with regard to Ireland in the most definite way from the policy of the ruling classes, until it not only makes common cause with the Irish, but actually takes the initiative in dissolving the Union established in 1801 and replacing it by a free federal relationship. And, indeed, this must be done, not as a matter of sympathy with Ireland, but as a demand made in the interests of the English proletariat. If not, the English people will remain tied to the leading-strings of the ruling classes, because it must join with them in a common front against Ireland. Every one of its movements in England itself is crippled by the disunion with the Irish, who form a very important section of the working class in England. *The primary condition* of emancipation here—the overthrow of the English landed oligarchy—remains impossible because its position here cannot be stormed so long as it maintains its strongly entrenched outposts in Ireland. But there, once affairs are in the hands of the Irish people itself, once it is made its own legislator and ruler, once it becomes autonomous, the abolition of the landed aristocracy (to a large extent the *same persons* as the English landlords) will be infinitely easier than here, because in Ireland it is not merely a simple economic question, but at the same time a *national* question, since the landlords there are not like those in England, the traditional dignitaries and representatives, but are the mortally hated oppressors of a nation. And not only does England's internal social development remain crippled by her present relation with Ireland; her foreign policy, and particularly her policy with regard to Russia and America, suffers the same fate.

But since the English working class undoubtedly throws the decisive weight into the scale of social emancipation generally, the lever has to be applied here. As a matter of fact, the English republic under Cromwell met shipwreck in—Ireland. *Non bis in idem!* * The Irish have played a capital joke on the English government by electing the "convict felon" O'Donovan Rossa to Parliament. The government papers are already threatening a renewed suspension of the Habeas Corpus Act, a "renewed system of terror." In fact, England never has and never *can*—so

* *I.e.,* the same thing cannot happen twice.

long as the present relation lasts—rule Ireland otherwise than by the most abominable reign of terror and the most reprehensible corruption.

In France things are going well so far. On the one hand, the out-of-date demagogic and democratic bawlers of all shades are compromising themselves. On the other, Bonaparte is being driven along a path of concessions, on which he is certain to break his neck.

The *Observer* of yesterday (this weekly belongs to the Ministry) remarks with regard to the Eulenburg Scandal in the Prussian Chamber: Napoleon said: *"Grattez le Russe, et vous trouverez le Tartare."* * With regard to Prussia it is not necessary to scratch—to find the Russian.

À propos: Reich, Dr. Med., has the christian name of Edward and seems, from the preface to his book, to be still living in Gotha.

My best greetings to the Countess and Fränzchen.

Yours,

K. M.

Couldn't we have the Bielefeld *Freiligrath Festbroschüre.***

---

* Scratch the Russian, and you will find the Tartar.
** A Freiligrath Jubilee pamphlet published in Bielefeld.

Dear Kugelmann,

Yesterday, for the first time for a long time, I went out into
the fresh air.

First of all business. Be so kind as to send *at once* a copy of
Vogt to Ascher and Co., Unter den Linden 11, Berlin. I should
be glad if, in despatching the book, you would get a receipt
from the post office and send it on to me. You would also oblige
me if you could let me know when, roughly, K. Hirsch wrote to
you about the *Vogt*.

The pamphlet which you sent me is one of the *plaidoyers* * with
which the privileged classes of the German-Russian-Baltic provinces are at the present time appealing to German sympathy.
These *canaille*, who have always distinguished themselves by
their zeal in the service of the Russian diplomats, army and police and who, since the transference of the provinces from Poland to Russia, have willingly bartered their nationality for the
legal authorisation to exploit the peasantry, are now crying out
because they see their privileged position endangered. The old
system of estates, orthodox Lutheranism and the exploitation of
the peasants is what they call German culture, the protection of
which Europe is now to take in hand. Hence, too, the last word
of this pamphlet—*landed property as the basis of civilisation*,
and landed property, moreover, as the wretched pamphleteer
himself admits, mainly consisting of directly manorial estates or
of peasant holdings *subject to tribute*.

In his quotations—in so far as they deal with Russian communal property—the fellow shows his ignorance as well as the
cloven hoof. Schedo Ferroti is one of the fellows who attribute
(in the interest of landlordism, of course) the pitiful position
of the Russian peasant to the existence of communal property,
just as, formerly, the *abolition of serfdom* in Western Europe—
instead of the serf's loss of his land—was decried as the cause
of pauperism. The Russian book *Land and Freedom* is of the
same calibre. Its author is a Baltic cabbage-junker called *Von
Lilienthal*. What impoverishes the Russian peasantry is what im-
poverished the French under Louis XIV, etc.—*state taxes and*

* Pleas.

obrok * *to the great landowners.* Instead of causing misery, *communal property* has been the only factor mitigating it.

It is, moreover, historically false to say that *communal property is Mongolian.* As I have repeatedly indicated in my writings, it is of Indian origin and is therefore to be found among all civilised European peoples in the early stages of their development. The specifically Slavic (not Mongolian) form in Russia (which is also found among the non-Russian South Slavs) bears in fact greatest similarity, *mutatis mutandis,* ** to the *old German modification* of Indian communal property.

That the Pole *Duchinski* in Paris should declare the Great Russian race to be not *Slavic,* but *Mongolian,* and should have tried to prove this with a great show of erudition, was to be expected from the standpoint of a Pole. Nevertheless, his contention is not correct. It is not the Russian peasantry, but the Russian nobility, which is strongly alloyed with Mongolian-Tartar elements. *Henri Martin,* the Frenchman, took the theory from Duchinski and "the inspired Gottfried Kinkel" has translated Martin and has thrust himself forward as an ardent friend of Poland, in order to make the democratic party forget his servile homage to Bismarck.

That, on the other hand, the Russian state, as against Europe and America, in its policy represents *Mongolism,* is of course a truth that has by now become a commonplace and therefore accessible even to people like Gottfried and the Baltic cabbage-junkers, philistines, priests and professors. The Baltic-German outcry must, therefore, in spite of everything, be exploited, because it puts the great German power, *Prussia,* in a "ticklish" position. Everything that arouses antipathy on our part towards those "representatives of German culture" is, precisely on that account, deemed worthy of protection in the eyes of Prussia. Another example of the crass ignorance of the pamphleteer: In his opinion the abandonment of Russian possessions in North America was merely a diplomatic trick on the part of the Russian government, which, be it remarked in passing, was very hard

---

* Quit rent.
** Having changed what must be changed.

pressed for costs. But the main point is this: the American Congress has recently published the documents relating to the transaction. These include, among other things, a report of the American envoy in which he writes explicitly to Washington: The acquisition is in the meantime not worth a cent *economically*, but—but thereby England is cut off from the sea on one side through the Yankees and the reversion of the whole of British North America to the U. St. is accelerated. That's the secret of the whole affair!

I approved of the substance of your correspondence with Jacoby, but the exaggerated praises of my activities have really shocked me. *Est modus in rebus!* * If you must praise, then old Jacoby ** himself is very praiseworthy. What other old radical in Europe possesses the sincerity and courage to place himself so decidedly on the side of the proletarian movement? That his transition measures and detailed proposals are of little value is an entirely unimportant matter. Between ourselves—take all in all—I expect more for the social movement from Germany than from France.

I have had a big row with that intriguer Bakunin. But more about that in my next letter.

My best compliments to Madame la Comtesse and Fränzchen.

Yours,

K. M.

---

* There is a measure in all things.
** Johann Jacoby, on January 20, 1870, made a speech on the "aims of the workers movement," in which he proclaimed his sympathy with it.

March 26, 1870.

Dear Kugelmann,

I am only writing a few lines today because just at the moment when I get ready to write to you again after so long a time, there is a Frenchman coming whom I shall not get rid of this afternoon, and the post goes at 5:30.

But tomorrow is Sunday and therefore a good Christian like myself is allowed to interrupt his work and to write you a long letter, particularly about the Russian case, which has taken a pretty turn.

Jennychen, our illustrious J. Williams, has a very good edition of father Goethe. By the by, she was invited a short time ago to Madame Vivanti's, the wife of a rich Italian merchant. There was a great *assemblée,** including a number of English people. Jennychen had a brilliant success with Shakespearean recitation.

Will you please greet Madame la Comtesse from me and thank her for the kind words that she was good enough to write. She has not the least cause to regret having preferred Latin to French. That not only reveals a taste at once classic and highly cultivated, but also explains why Madame never reaches the end of her Latin.

Best greetings to Fränzchen.

Mohr.**

---

* Assembly.
** Mohr—Moor, a nickname given to Marx because of his dark complexion.

March 28, 1870.

Dear Kugelmann,

As I have an abscess on the right thigh which makes sitting for any length of time impossible, I am sending you the enclosed *letter for the Brunswick Comité,* * Bracke and Co.*, instead of writing twice. It would be best if, after reading it through, you could hand the letter over personally and remind them again that the information is *confidential*, not intended for the public.

[The enclosed letter reads:]

International Workingmen's Association,
Central Council, London.

Confidential Information.

The Russian Bakunin (although I have known him since 1843, I shall here ignore everything not absolutely necessary for the understanding of what follows) met Marx in London shortly after the foundation of the *International*. There the latter took him into the Association, for which Bakunin promised to work to the best of his ability. Bakunin went to Italy and received there from Marx the *Provisional Statutes* and *Address to the Working Classes*, answered "very enthusiastically," did nothing. After some years, during which nothing was heard from him, he turned up again in Switzerland. There he joined, not the *International*, but the *Ligue de la paix et de la liberté*.** After the Congress of this peace league (Geneva 1867) Bakunin got on to its *executive committee*, but found opponents there, who not only denied him any "dictatorial" influence, but watched him closely as being "suspect as a Russian." Shortly after the Brussels Congress of the *International* (September 1868) the *Peace League* held its congress at Lausanne. Here Bakunin acted the firebrand and—be it re-marked *en passant* ***—denounced the occidental bourgeoisie in the tone in which Muscovite optimists are accustomed to attack western civilisation —to palliate their own barbarism. He proposed a number of resolutions, which, absurd in themselves, were intended to instil fear into the bourgeois cretins and allow Monsieur Bakunin to leave the Peace League and enter the International with *éclat*. It suffices to note that the programme proposed by Bakunin to the Lausanne Congress contains such absurdities as the *"equality of classes," "abolition of the right of inheritance as the first step* in the social revolution," etc. Empty babblings, a garland of hollow fancies claiming to be horrifying, in short an insipid improvisation, calculated to make a certain effect. Bakunin's friends in Paris (where a Russian has a seat on the editorial board of the *Revue Positiviste*) and in London proclaim to the world Bakunin's exit from the Peace League as *un evéne-*

* Committee.
** League of Peace and Liberty.
*** In passing.

*ment** and declare his grotesque programme—that *olla potrida*** of outworn platitudes—wonderfully awe-inspiring and original.

Bakunin meanwhile had joined the *Branche Romande*** of the *International* (in Geneva). It took him years to decide upon this step. But it did not take days for Monsieur Bakunin to decide to transform the *International* into an instrument *of his own.*

Behind the back of the London General Council—which was informed only when everything was already arranged—he founded the so-called *Alliance des Démocrats Socialistes.***** The programme of this society was none other than that proposed by Bakunin at the Lausanne Peace Congress. The Society thereby proclaimed itself from the outset as a propaganda body of the specifically Bakuninist cult and Bakunin himself, *one of the most ignorant men in the field of social theory,* appeared as the *founder of a sect.* The theoretical programme of the Alliance was however pure farce. The serious aspect of the affair lay in its practical organisation. This society was to be *international,* with its Central Committee in *Geneva,* that is, under Bakunin's personal direction. At the same time it was to be an *integral* part of the *International Workingmen's Association.* Its branches were to be represented at the next congress of the International (in Bâsle) and were at the same time to hold their own Congress in separate sittings, etc., etc., *side by side with the other.*

The human material which at first stood at Bakunin's disposal consisted of the majority of the *Comité Fédéral Romand***** of the International at that time (in Geneva). J. P. Becker, whose propagandist zeal at times runs away with his head, was pushed forward to the front of the stage. In Italy and Spain Bakunin had a few allies.

The General Council in London was fully informed. However, it let Bakunin proceed undisturbed up to the moment when he found it necessary to send the General Council through Becker, the statutes (and programme) of the *Alliance des Démocrats Socialistes* for ratification. The General Council answered with a thoroughly reasoned resolution—wholly "judicial" and "objective" in tone, but ironic in its "considerations"—which concluded in the following manner.

1. The General Council does *not* admit the Alliance *as a branch* of the International.

2. All the paragraphs of the Statutes of the Alliance referring to its relations with the *International* are declared *null and void.*

The "considerations" for this resolution demonstrated clearly and forcefully that the *Alliance* was nothing but an instrument to disorganise the *International.*

The blow was unexpected. Bakunin had already made the *Égalité,* central organ of the French speaking members of the *International* in Switzerland, his *own* organ, and had, in addition started at Locle a little private journal of his own, the *Progrès.* The *Progrès* is playing this role up to today under the editorship of a fanatical adherent of Bakunin, a certain Guillaume.

After several weeks' reflection the Central Committee of the Alliance

* An event.
** Mixed dish.
*** Romande—Romance, *i.e.,* belonging to the Neo-Latin people.
**** Alliance of Socialist Democrats.
***** Romance Federal Committee.

sent its answer to the General Council, over the signature of Perron, a Genevese. In its eagerness to serve the good cause, the Alliance was ready *to sacrifice its independent organisation*, but on one condition—namely, that the General Council recognise its *"radical" principles*.

The General Council replied: It was not its function to sit in judgment on the theoretic value of the programmes of its various sections. It had only to see that those programmes contained nothing directly contradictory to the letter and spirit of the Statutes. It must therefore insist upon the absurd phrase about the *égalité des classes*,* being struck from the pro- gramme of the Alliance and being replaced by the *abolition des classes* ** (which was done). For the rest, after *dissolving its own independent inter- national organisation*, the alliance could enter the International after having supplied the General Council with a full list of its branches (which, *nota bene*, was not done).

The incident was therewith closed. *Nominally*, the *Alliance* dissolved it- self; *actually*, it remained in existence, under Bakunin's leadership, he at the same time controlled the Genevese *Comité Romand Fédéral* of the *International*. To its former press organs were added the *Conféderation* of Barcelona and, after the Bâsle Congress, the Naples *Equalita*.

Bakunin now attempted to reach his goal—the transformation of the *International* into his personal instrument—by other means. Through our *Comité Romand* at Geneva he proposed to the General Council the inclu- sion of the "inheritance question" in the Agenda of the Bâsle Congress. The General Council agreed, in order to be able to deal a direct blow to Bakunin. Bakunin's plan was this: the Bâsle Congress, in accepting the principles (!) put forward by Bakunin at Lausanne, will show the world that it is not Bakunin who has come over to the International, but the Inter- national that has gone over to Bakunin. Obvious results, the London Gen- eral Council (of whose hostility to the warming up of this obsolete St. Simonism Bakunin was fully aware) would have to resign and the Bâsle Congress would *transfer the General Council to Geneva*, that is, the Inter- national would come under the Dictatorship of Bakunin.

Bakunin set a complete conspiracy going to secure a majority at the Bâsle Congress. Even *false* mandates were not lacking, such as Monsieur Guillaume's mandate for Locle. Bakunin himself begged mandates from Naples and Lyons. Every kind of slander against the General Council was spread abroad. Some were told that the bourgeois element dominated the Council, others that it was the seat of *Communisme autoritaire*.***

The results of the Bâsle Congress are well known. Bakunin's proposals were not accepted and the General Council remained in London.

The annoyance which followed this failure—perhaps Bakunin had based all kinds of private speculations on the assumption of success—found ex- pression in the *Égalité* and *Progrès*. These papers meanwhile were assum- ing more and more the guise of an official oracle. Now one, now another Swiss Section of the International was excommunicated because, in opposi- tion to Bakunin's explicit instructions, it had taken part in the political movement, etc. Finally the rage against the General Council, so long restrained, broke out openly. The *Égalité* and *Progrès* derided, attacked.

* Equality of classes.
** Abolition of classes.
*** Authoritarian Communism.

accused the General Council of not fulfilling its duties, for example in regard to the quarterly bulletin, the General Council must give up its direct control over England and allow an English Central Committee to be established, to deal with all English affairs, the resolutions of the General Council on the imprisoned Fenians went beyond its functions, since it has not to deal with questions of local politics. Moreover, the *Égalité* and *Progrès* took up the cudgels for *Schweitzer* and categorically demanded that the General Council declare itself officially and *publiquement* * on the Liebknecht-Schweitzer question. The Paris newspaper *Le Travail,* ** into which Schweitzer's Paris friends smuggled articles in his favour, was praised on that account by the *Égalité* and *Progrès,* the former calling upon the *Travail* to make common cause against the General Council.

The time had now come for action to be taken. What follows is an exact copy of the circular sent by the General Council to the Genevese *Comité Fédéral.* The document is too long for me to translate into German [original in French].

'*The General Council to the Conseil Fédéral de la Suisse Romande* *** *at Geneva.*

In its extraordinary session of January 1, 1870, the General Council resolved:
1. We read in the *Égalité* of December 11, 1869:
"It is certain that the General Council neglects matters of extreme importance. . . . We remind the General Council of its obligations under the first article of the Rules: 'The General Council is obliged to carry out the resolutions of Congress! We have enough questions to put to the General Council for its replies to make up a fairly long bulletin. They will come later. Meanwhile, etc. . . .'"

The General Council is aware of no article, either in the Statutes or the Rules, which *obliges* it to enter into correspondence or controversy with the *Égalité* or to make replies to the questions of any newspapers whatsoever.

The Federal Council of the *Suisse Romande* alone represents the branches of the *Suisse Romande* at the General Council. When the Federal Council addresses questions or reprimands to us through the only legitimate channel, that is to say through its secretary, the General Council will always be ready to reply. But the Federal Council has not the right either to abdicate its functions into the hands of the *Égalité* and the *Progrès,* or to allow these papers to usurp its functions.

Generally speaking, the correspondence of the General Council with the National and Local Committees cannot be published without doing great harm to the general interests of the Association. Consequently, if other organs of the International were to imitate the *Progrès* and the *Égalité,* the General Council would find itself confronted by the alternative of discrediting itself in the eyes of the public by keeping silence or of violating its duties by replying publicly.

The *Égalité* joins the *Progrès* in inviting the *Travail* to demand from the General Council an account of its actions; here we have almost a League of Public Welfare.****

* Publicly.
** *Labour.*
*** Federal Council of Romance Switzerland.
**** The League of Public Welfare was founded in 1863. Its programme consisted of demands for wide liberal reforms.

2. Assuming that the questions put by the *Égalité* proceed from the *Conseil Fédéral de la Suisse Romande*, we shall reply to them, but only on condition that such questions shall not in the future be communicated to us in the same way.

3. *The Question of a Bulletin.*

In the resolutions of the Lausanne Congress,* which are included in the rules, it is laid down that the National Committees shall send the General Council documents dealing with the proletarian movement and that the General Council shall thereupon publish a bulletin in the different languages "as often as its means permit." The obligation of the General Council was thus made dependent upon conditions which have never been fulfilled. Even the statistical enquiry prescribed by the statutes, ordered by several consecutive general congresses and demanded each year by the General Council, has never been made. As to its means, the General Council, would have long ceased to exist had it not been for local contributions from England and the personal sacrifices of its members.

Consequently the rule adopted at the Lausanne Congress has remained a dead letter. As to the Bâsle Congress,** it did not discuss the fulfilment of an existing resolution, but the possibility of publishing a bulletin, and on this question it passed no resolution.

For the rest, the General Council is of the opinion that the original demand for a public bulletin issued by it is at the present time fully met by the different organs of the International published in the different languages and exchanged for each other. It would be absurd to publish in costly bulletins what is already made public without expense to the General Council. On the other hand, a bulletin publishing material not contained in the organs of the International would merely serve to admit our enemies behind the scenes.

4. *Question of the formation of a regional Council for England.*

Long before the *Égalité* was founded this proposal was periodically made to the General Council by one or two of its English members. It has always been rejected practically unanimously.

Although the revolutionary initiative will probably come from France, England alone can serve as the lever of a serious economic revolution. It is the only country where there are no more peasants and where property in land is concentrated in a few hands. It is the only country where the capitalist form—that is to say combined labour on a large scale under capitalist employers—has invaded practically the whole of production. It is the only country where the great majority of the population consists of wage labourers. It is the only country where the class struggle and the organisation of the working class through the trade unions has acquired a certain degree of maturity and universality. As a result of its dominating position in the world market, it is the only country where every revolution in its economic conditions must react directly on the entire world. If this country is the classic seat of landlordism and capitalism, by virtue of that fact it is also here that the material conditions of their destruction are most highly developed. The General Council being at present placed in the happy position of having its hand directly on this great lever of the prole-

* The Lausanne Congress of the First International, September 2-8, 1867.

** The Bâsle Congress of the First International, September 6-8, 1869.

tarian revolution, it would be sheer folly, we would almost say it would be
an outright crime, to allow that hold to fall into purely English hands!

The English have all the material requisites necessary for the social
revolution. What they lack is the spirit of generalisation and revolutionary
ardour. It is only the General Council which can supply this deficiency,
which can thus accelerate the truly revolutionary movement in this country
and consequently everywhere. The great achievements which we have already
accomplished in this direction are borne witness to by the most intelligent
papers and those in the best standing among the ruling classes, for example
the *Pall Mall Gazette,* The *Saturday Review,* the *Spectator* and the *Fortnightly Review,* not to speak of the so-called radical members of the House
of Commons and House of Lords who, a short time ago, still wielded a
great influence over the leaders of the English workers. They accuse us
publicly of having poisoned and almost extinguished the English spirit of
the working class and of having forced it into revolutionary Socialism.

The only way to bring about this change is to act in the capacity of the
General Council of the International Association. As the General Council
we can initiate measures (such, for example, as the foundation of the Land
and Labour League), which later, in the public execution of their tasks,
appear as spontaneous movements of the English working class.

If a Regional Council were formed apart from the General Council what
would be the immediate effect? Placed between the General Council of the
International and the General Council of the trade unions, the Regional
Council would have no authority whatever. On the other hand the General
Council would lose its control of the great lever. If we had preferred the
éclat of the market-place to serious and unostentatious work, we would
perhaps have made this mistake of answering publicly the question of the
Égalité as to why "the General Council submits to this burdensome accumulation of functions."

England cannot be treated simply as one country among a number of
other countries. She must be treated as the metropolis of capitalism.

5. *Question of the Resolutions of the General Council on the Irish Amnesty.*

If England is the bulwark of European landlordism and capitalism, the
only point at which the great blow against official England can be struck
is Ireland.

In the first place, Ireland is the bulwark of English landlordism. If it
falls in Ireland, it will fall in England. In Ireland the operation is a hundred times more easy, because there the economic struggle is *concentrated
exclusively against landed property,* because there the struggle is at the
same time a *national* struggle, and because the people there are more revolutionary and more exasperated than in England. Landlordism in Ireland
is maintained solely by the English Army. The moment the compulsory
union of the two countries ceases to exist, a social revolution, although in
antiquated forms, will break out in Ireland. English landlordism will not
only lose a source of its great wealth, but also its greatest moral force,
that is to say, its capacity to represent England's dominion over Ireland.
On the other hand, in supporting the power of its landlords in Ireland,
the English proletariat makes them invulnerable in England itself.

Secondly, the English bourgeoisie has not only exploited Irish poverty to
keep down, by the forced immigration of the poor Irish, the wages of the
English workers, it has also divided the proletariat into two hostile camps.

The revolutionary ardour of the Celtic labourer does not mix with the solid but slow nature of the Anglo-Saxon worker. Indeed, in all the great industrial centres of England there exists a profound antagonism between the Irish and the English working man. The average English worker hates the Irish working man as a competitor who lowers his wages and his standard of life. He entertains towards the Irishman national and religious antipathies, regarding him much as the poor white of the Southern States of North America regarded the black slaves. This antagonism among the proletarians of England is artificially encouraged and fed by the bourgeoisie, who know that this cleavage is the real secret of the maintenance of their power.

This antagonism repeats itself on the other side of the Atlantic. Driven off their native soil by sheep and cattle, the Irish find a new home in the United States, where they represent a considerable and growing proportion of the population. Their sole idea, their sole passion, is hatred of the English. The English government and the American government—that is to say the classes which they represent—feed these sentiments in order to perpetuate the international antagonisms which prevent any serious and sincere alliance between the working classes of the two countries, and, consequently, their common emancipation.

Ireland offers to the English government the only pretext for maintaining a larger permanent army which, in case of need, can be despatched against the English workers, as we have seen, after having completed its military training in Ireland. Finally, what ancient Rome demonstrated on an enormous scale is being repeated in our day in England. The people which oppresses another people forges its own chains.

The position of the International Association with regard to the Irish question is thus quite clear. Its first concern is to forward the social revolution in England. To do this, the decisive blow must be struck in Ireland.

The resolutions of the General Council on the Irish Amnesty are intended to serve as an introduction to other resolutions which will proclaim that, quite apart from any idea of international justice, it is essential to the emancipation of the English working class to transform the present compulsory union—that is to say, the slavery of Ireland—into an equal and free confederation, if this is possible, into complete separation, if that must need be.

For the rest, the doctrines of the *Égalité* and the *Progrès* on the connection or rather the absence of connection between the social and the political movement have never, as far as we are aware, been recognised by any of our Congresses. They are contrary to our Statutes. The Statutes say:

"That economic emancipation is the great end *to which every political movement is to be subordinated as a means!*"

These words—"as a means"—were suppressed in the French translation prepared in 1864 by the Paris Committee. Questioned by the General Council, the Paris Committee put forward as an excuse the difficulties of its political position.

The authentic text of the Statutes was mutilated in other ways. The first part of the preamble of the Statute reads:

"That the struggle for the emancipation of the working class is . . . a struggle . . . for equal rights and duties, and for the abolition of all class rule. . . ."

The French translation has "equal rights and duties"—that is to say, it employs the general phrase which can be found in practically every democratic manifesto for the last century, and which has a different meaning on the lips of different classes—but omits the concrete demand for the "abolition of all class rule."

Further, we read in the second paragraph of the preamble of the Statutes:

"That the economic subjection of the *labourer* to the *appropriator of the means of labour*, that is, of the sources of life, etc."

The Parisian version has "capital" as the translation of "the means of labour, that is, of the sources of life," although the latter expression includes the land as well as the remaining means of production.

The original and authentic text was restored in the French translation published in Brussels in 1866.

6. *Liebknecht-Schweitzer Question*.

The *Égalité* says: "Both these groups belong to the International." This is false. The Eisenachers' group (which the *Progrès* and the *Égalité* are anxious to portray as Citizen Liebknecht's group) belongs to the International. Schweitzer's group does not.

Schweitzer himself has explained at great length in his paper, *Der Sozialdemokrat*, why the Lassallean organisation cannot affiliate with the International without destroying itself. Unwittingly, he has told the truth. His artificial *sectarian* organisation stands in opposition to the *real* organisation of the working *class*.

The *Progrès* and the *Égalité* have invited the General Council to express publicly its "opinion" on the personal differences between Liebknecht and Schweitzer. As Citizen J. Ph. Becker (who is slandered just as much as Liebknecht in Schweitzer's paper) is a member of the editorial board of the *Égalité*, it appears truly strange that its editors are not better informed about the facts. They should know that Liebknecht, in the *Demokratisches Wochenblatt*, publicly invited Schweitzer to accept the General Council as arbitrator of their differences and that Schweitzer no less publicly repudiated the authority of the General Council.

The General Council has made every effort to put an end to this scandal. It ordered its Secretary for Germany to write to Schweitzer, which was done, but all attempts of the General Council to advise him were frustrated by Schweitzer's firm resolve to maintain at any price his autocratic power within sectarian organisation.

The General Council will decide the favorable moment when its public intervention in this quarrel will do more good than harm.

By order of the General Council, etc.

London, 16. 1, 1870.

The French Committees (although Bakunin had been actively intriguing in Lyons and Marseilles and had won over a few young hotheads), as well as the *Conseil Général Belge* * (Brussels), have *fully endorsed* this circular of the General Council.

The copy for Geneva was delayed somewhat because *Jung*, Secretary for Switzerland, was very busy. It therefore crossed an official letter from *Perret*, Secretary of the Geneva *Comité Fédéral Romand*, to the General Council.

* Belgian General Council.

The crisis had broken out in Geneva before the arrival of our letter. Some members of the editorial board of the *Égalité* had opposed the policy dictated by Bakunin. Bakunin and his followers (including six members of the board) wanted to force the Geneva Central Committee to dismiss the unruly members. The Geneva Committee, however, had long grown tired of Bakunin's despotism and saw itself with great displeasure being forced by him into opposition to the other German-Swiss Committees, the General Council, etc. It therefore endorsed the attitude of those members of the editorial board who had opposed Bakunin. Thereupon Bakunin's six followers on the *Égalité* resigned, hoping thereby to put an end to the publication of the paper.

In answer to our letter the Geneva Central Committee declared that the attacks in the *Égalité* had been made without its approval, that it had never endorsed the policy preached therein and that in future the paper would be strictly supervised by the Committee, etc.

Bakunin thereupon retired from Geneva to Tessin. As far as Switzerland is concerned, he now controls only the *Progrès* (Locle).

Shortly afterward *Herzen* died. Bakunin, who from the time that he decided to set up as *director of the European labour movement* had denied his old friend and patron Herzen, hastened to sing his praises immediately after his death. Why? Herzen, though personally wealthy, allowed the pseudo-socialist, pan-slavist party in Russia, which was friendly towards him, to pay him 25,000 francs annually for purposes of propaganda. By his pæan of praise Bakunin directed this stream of money *to himself* and— *malgré sa haine de l'héritage* *—thereby entered financially and morally upon the "Herzen *heritage*" *sine beneficio inventarii.***

At the same time a colony of young Russian refugees had settled in Geneva, students whose intentions are really honest and whose sincerity is proved by the adoption of the *fight against panslavism* as the chief point of their programme.

They have a paper in Geneva called *La Voix du Peuple.****

About two weeks ago they applied to London, sent in their Programme and Statutes, and requested permission to form a Russian branch. Permission was given.

In a separate letter to Marx they asked him to represent them provisionally on the General Council. That too was done. At the same time they indicated—and apparently *wish to excuse themselves* to Marx on this account—that in the immediate future they would have to expose Bakunin publicly, since he spoke in two entirely different tongues, one in Russia, another in Europe.

The game of this very dangerous intriguer—at least in the domain of the International—will soon be played out.

---

* Despite his hatred of inheritance.
** Without benefit of inventory.
*** *The Voice of the People.*

Dear King Wenceslas!

I returned to London this week after a month's stay in Manchester and found your letter awaiting me.

I cannot tell you when I will be leaving, not even answer the question—which you did not ask—whether I shall go at all.

Last year I counted upon a second edition of my book, and consequently upon receiving some money for the first edition. But you see from the enclosed letter from Meissner, which came today, that all this is still a thing of the future. (Please send me the letter back.)

The German professorial worthies have recently found themselves obliged to take notice of me here and there, even if in a stupid fashion. For example, A. Wagner in a booklet on landed property and Held (Bonn) in one on the agricultural credit system in the Rhine province.

Herr Lange (*Ueber die Arbeiterfrage, etc.*, 2. Edition) sings my praises loudly, but with the object of making himself important. Herr Lange, you see, has made a great discovery. The whole of history can be brought under a single great natural law. This natural law is the *phrase* (in this application Darwin's expression becomes nothing but a phrase) "the struggle for life," and the content of this phrase is the Malthusian law of population or, rather, over-population. So, instead of analysing the struggle for life as represented historically in varying and definite forms of society, all that has to be done is to translate every concrete struggle into the phrase, "struggle for life," and this phrase itself into the Malthusian population fantasy. One must admit that this is a very impressive method—for swaggering, sham-scientific, bombastic ignorance and intellectual laziness.

What the same Lange says about the Hegelian method and my application of it is really childish. First of all, he understands nothing about Hegel's method and secondly, as a consequence, even less about my critical application of it. In one respect he reminds me of Moses Mendelssohn. That prototype of a windbag wrote to Lessing, asking how he could possibly take the "dead dog Spinoza" *au sérieux!* * Similarly Herr Lange wonders that

* Seriously.

Engels, I, and others take the dead dog Hegel *au sérieux*, after Büchner, Lange, Dr. Dühring, Fechner, etc., have long since agreed that they—poor deer *—have buried him long ago. Lange is naive enough to say that I "move with rare freedom" in empirical matter. He hasn't the least idea that this "free movement in matter" is nothing but a paraphrase for the *method* of dealing with matter—that is, the *dialectic method*.

My best thanks to Madame la Comtesse for her kind note. It really does one good at a time "when more and more of the good are vanishing." But, speaking seriously, I am always glad when some lines from your dear wife remind me of the happy days I spent in your circle.

As to Meissner's pressure for the second volume, I have not only been interrupted by illness throughout the winter; I also found it necessary to learn Russian, because in dealing with the land question it became essential to go to the original sources in studying the relations of Russian landed property. Moreover, in connection with the Irish land question, the English government published a series of blue books (soon concluded) on the land question in all countries. Finally—*entre nous* **—I wanted the second edition of the first volume to appear first. If that were to come while I was finishing the second volume it would only disturb my work.

Best compliments on Jenny's part and to all the members of the Kugelmann family.

Yours,

K. M.

* Marx's English.
** Between ourselves.

London, September 14, 1870.

Dear Wenceslas,

The *Address* * enclosed.

My time is so taken up with "International" work that I do not get to bed before three in the morning. This to excuse my obstinate silence.

Best greetings to Madame la Comtesse and Fränzchen.

Yours,

K. M.

---

* The second Address of the General Council of the First International on the Franco-Prussian War, dated September 9, 1870.

London, December 13, 1870.

Dear Kugelmann,

You must explain my long silence by the fact that during the war, which has taken most of the foreign correspondents of the General Council to France, I have had to conduct *practically the entire international correspondence*, which is no trifle. Apart from that with the *"postal freedom"* prevailing now in Germany and particularly in the North German Confederation, and very "particularly" in Hanover, it is dangerous—not for me, it is true, but for my German correspondents—for me to write them my opinion of the war, and what else can one write about at the present moment?

For example, you ask me for our first *Address* on the war. I had sent it to you. It has obviously been confiscated. In this letter I am enclosing the two *Addresses* issued as a pamphlet as well as Professor Beesly's article in the *Fortnightly Review* and today's *Daily News*. Since this paper has a Prussian tinge, the things will probably get through. Professor Beesly is a Comtist and is as such obliged to support all sorts of crotchets, but for the rest a very capable and brave man. He is professor of history at London University.

It seems that Germany was not satisfied with capturing Bonaparte, his generals and his army; with them, imperialism too, with all its infirmities, has acclimatised itself in the land of the oak and the linden.

As to the German bourgeois, I am not at all suprised by his thirst for conquest. First of all, to seize things is the vital principle of every bourgeoisie and to take foreign provinces is after all "taking." And then the German citizen has dutifully accepted so many kicks from his sovereigns, and particularly from the Hohenzollerns, that it must be a real pleasure to him when, for a change, those kicks are administered to the foreigner.

In any case this war has freed us from the "bourgeois republicans." It has put a horrible end to that crew. And that is an important result. It has given our professors the best opportunity of damning themselves in the eyes of the whole world as servile pedants. The results which will follow are the best propaganda for our principles.

Here in England public opinion on the outbreak of war was ultra-Prussian; it has now turned into the opposite. In the cafés chantants for example the German singers with their Wi-Wa-Watch on the Rhine have been hissed off while French singers with the Marseillaise have been accompanied in chorus. Apart from the decided sympathy of the mass of the people for the Republic and the anger of the respectable people about the alliance between Russia and Prussia—now clear as daylight—and the shameless tone of Prussian diplomacy since the military successes, the way in which the war has been conducted—the requisitioning system, the setting fire to villages, the shooting of franctireurs, the taking of hostages and similar recapitulations of the Thirty Years' War—all this has aroused universal indignation. Of course, the English have done the same in India, Jamaica, etc., but the French are neither Hindus, nor Chinese, nor Negroes, and the Prussian is not a heavenborn Englishman. It is a truly Hohenzollern idea that a people commits a crime in continuing to defend itself once its regular army has disappeared. In fact, the war of the Prussian people against Napoleon I was a real thorn in the side of the brave Friedrich Wilhelm III, as you can see from Professor Pertz's story of Gneisenau, who made the war of franctireurs into a system through his *Landsturm* * organisation. The fact that the people fought on their own initiative and independent of the all-highest's order gave Friedrich Wilhelm III, no peace.

However, the last word has not yet been spoken. The war in France can still take a very "unpleasant" turn. The resistance put up by the Loire Army was "beyond" calculation, and the present scattering of the Prussian forces right and left is merely to instil fear, but in fact only results in awakening the power of defence at every point and weakening the offensive force. The threatened bombardment of Paris is also a trick. On the town of Paris itself it can, by all the rules of probability, have no serious effect. If a few outworks are destroyed, a few breaches made, what help is that when the besieged outnumber the besiegers? And if the besieged made exceptionally good sorties, when the enemy defends himself behind entrenchments, how much better would they not fare, when the roles are reversed?

* Army reserve.

To starve Paris out is the only real way. But if that is delayed long enough to allow armies to be formed and the people's war to develop in the provinces, even that will do nothing except transfer the centre of gravity. Moreover, even after the surrender of Paris, which cannot be held and kept quiet by a mere handful, a large part of the invaders would be maintained in idleness.

But however the war may end, it has given the French proletariat practice in arms, and that is the best guarantee of the future.

The shameless tone which Russia and Prussia adopt towards England may have wholly unexpected and unpleasant results for them. The matter stands like this: By the Paris Peace Treaty of 1856 England *disarmed herself.* England is a sea power and can counterpose to the great Continental military powers only the weapon of naval warfare. The certain method is temporarily to destroy or bring to a standstill, the overseas trade of the continental powers. This mainly depends on operating the principle of seizing enemy goods in neutral vessels. This maritime right (as well as other similar rights) was surrendered by England in the so-called Declaration attached to the Paris Treaty. Clarendon did this at the secret order of the Russian Palmerston. The Declaration, however, is not an integral part of the treaty itself and has *never* been legally ratified in England. The Russian and Prussian gentlemen are reckoning without their host if they imagine that the influence of the Queen, who is Prussianised from family interest, and the bourgeois weak-mindedness of a Gladstone, would at a decisive moment keep John Bull from throwing this self-created "charming obstacle" overboard. And he can always strangle Russian-German sea trade in a few weeks. We shall then have an opportunity of studying the long faces of the Petersburg and Berlin diplomats, and the still longer faces of the "power patriots." *Qui vivra verra.*[*]

My best compliments to Madame la Comtesse and Fränzchen.

Yours,

K. M.

À propos. Can you let me have Windthorst's various Reichstag Speeches?

---

[*] He who lives will see.

London, February 14, 1871.

Dear Kugelmann,

I am sorry to learn from your last letter that your state of health has again got worse. In the autumn and winter months mine was tolerable, although the cough which I contracted during my last stay in Hanover is still troubling me.

I sent you the *Daily News* containing my letter. Obviously it has been confiscated, like the other things I sent you. Today I am enclosing the cutting, as well as the first Address of the General Council. The letter actually contains nothing but facts, but is effective precisely because of that.

You know my opinion of the middle-class heroes. Monsieur Jules Favre (notorious from the days of the Provisional Government and Cavaignac) and Co. have, however, surpassed my expectations. First of all they allowed the *"sabre orthodox,"* the *"crétin militaire,"* as Blanqui rightly dubs Trochu, to carry out his "plan." This plan consisted simply in prolonging the *passive resistance* of Paris to the utmost limit, that is, to starvation point, and of confining the offensive to sham manoeuvres and *des sorties platoniques.** I am not guessing all this. I know the contents of a letter which Jules Favre himself wrote to Gambetta, and in which he complains that he and other members of that part of the government cowering in Paris sought in vain to spur Trochu on to serious offensive measures. Trochu always answered that that would give the upper hand to Parisian demagogy. Gambetta replied: *Vous avez prononcé votre propre condamnation.*** Trochu considered it much more important to keep down the Reds in Paris with the help of his Breton bodyguard—which renders him the same service that the Corsicans rendered Louis Bonaparte— than to defeat the Prussians. This is the real secret of the defeats not only at Paris, but throughout France, where the bourgeoisie, in agreement with the majority of the local authorities, have acted on the same principle.

After Trochu's plan had been carried out to its climax—to the point where Paris had to surrender or starve—Jules Favre and Co. had only to follow the example of the commander of the

* Platonic sorties.
** You have pronounced your own condemnation.

fortress at Toul. He did not surrender. He merely explained to the Prussians that he was compelled through lack of food to abandon the defence and open the gates of the fortress. They could now do as they chose.

But Jules Favre is not content with signing a formal surrender. Having declared himself, his governmental colleagues and Paris the King of Prussia's *prisoners of war,* he has the audacity *to act in the name of the whole of France.* What did he know of the situation in France outside Paris? Absolutely nothing, except what Bismarck was gracious enough to tell him.

More. These *Messieurs les prisoniers du roi de Prusse** go further and declare that that part of the French government still free in Bordeaux has outlived its mandate and can only act *in agreement* with them—the *prisoners of war of the Prussian King.* Since they, as prisoners of war, can themselves only act at the command of their war-lord, they thereby proclaim the King of Prussia *de facto* the highest authority in France.

Even Louis Bonaparte, after he surrendered and was taken prisoner at Sedan, was not so shameless. To Bismarck's proposals he replied that he could not enter upon negotiations because as a Prussian prisoner he had ceased to exercise any authority in France. At the most Favre could have accepted a *conditional* armistice for the whole of France, with the proviso, namely, that it should be sanctioned by the Bordeaux Government, which alone had the right and the capacity to agree upon the clauses of such an armistice with the Prussians. They, at any rate, would not have allowed the latter to exclude the *eastern* war area from the armistice. They would not have allowed the Prussians to round off so advantageously for them their line of occupation.

Rendered impudent by the pretensions of his prisoners' of war, who in that capacity continued to play at being the French government, Bismarck is now freely interfering in internal French affairs. He protests, the noble fellow, against Gambetta's decree concerning the general elections to the *Assemblée,*** because the decree is prejudicial to the freedom of the elections. Indeed! Gambetta should answer with a protest against the state of siege

---

* Gentlemen, prisoners of the King of Prussia.
** Assembly.

and other circumstances in Germany, which annihilate the freedom of the elections to the Reichstag.

I hope that Bismarck sticks to his conditions of peace. Four
hundred million pounds sterling as war indemnity—half the
English national debt! Even the French bourgeoisie will understand that. They will perhaps at last realise that by continuing
the war they could at the worst *only gain.*

The mob, high class and low, judges by appearances, by the
façade, the immediate result. During the last twenty years it has,
all over the world, apotheosised Louis Bonaparte. I have always
exposed him, even at his apogee, as a *mediocre canaille.* That is
also my opinion of the *Junker* Bismarck. Nevertheless, I do not
consider Bismarck so stupid as he would be if his diplomacy
were voluntary. The man is caught by the Russian Chancellery in
a net which only a lion could tear through, and he is no lion.

For example, Bismarck's demand that France should hand over
her twenty best ships and Pondicherry in India! Such an idea
could not emanate from a really Prussian diplomat. He would
know that a Prussian Pondicherry would be nothing but a Prussian hostage in English hands; that England, if she wanted to,
could seize the twenty warships before they enter the Baltic Sea
and that such demands could only have the object, absurd from
the Prussian point of view, of making John Bull distrustful before the Prussians are out of the French wood.

But Russia is interested precisely in such a result, in order to
secure still more firmly Prussia's allegiance. In fact these demands have given rise to a complete change of feeling even in
the peace-loving English middle class. Everybody is now calling
for war. This provocative act and this danger to its interests are
making even the bourgeois mad. It is more than probable that,
thanks to the *Prussian "wisdom,"* Gladstone and Co. will be
kicked out of office and supplanted by a ministry declaring war
against Prussia.

On the other hand things look pretty bad in Russia. Since Wilhelm became an Emperor, the old Muscovite, anti-German party,
with the heir to the throne at its head, has again won the upper
hand completely. And it is supported by the sentiments of the
people. Gorchakov's subtle policy is incomprehensible to them.

It is therefore probable that the tsar will either have to change his foreign policy altogether, or be obliged to kick the bucket, like his predecessors Alexander I, Paul and Peter III.

With a simultaneous convulsion in the politics of England and Russia, where would Prussia be, at a moment when its northern and southeastern frontiers are left defenceless against invasion and Germany's defensive strength is exhausted? Not to forget that since the outbreak of war Prussia-Germany has sent 1,500,000 men to France, of whom only about 700,000 are still on their legs.

Despite all appearance to the contrary, Prussia's position is anything but pleasant.

If France holds out, uses the armistice to reorganise her army and finally gives the war a really revolutionary character—and the artful Bismarck is doing his best to this end—the new German, Borussian* Empire may still get a quite unexpected thrashing as its baptism.

My best compliments to the Countess and Fränzchen.

Yours,

K. M.

A propos: You wrote me once about a book by Haxthausen on Westphalian (I think) conditions of landownership. I should be glad if you would send it to me.

Be so good as to forward the enclosure to Dr. Jacoby (Königsberg) but *stamp* it by way of precaution.

Get your wife to write on the enclosed letter the address of Dr. Johann Jacoby, Königsberg.

Jennychen has just asked me to send her greetings to "Trautchen, Fränzchen and Wenzelchen," which I hereby do.

[Enclosed with this letter was the following cutting from the *Daily News,* containing a letter from Marx, dated January 16, 1871, and published under the heading: *Freedom of the Press and of Speech in Germany*:]

To the Editor of the Daily News:
Sir,

In accusing the French Government of "having rendered impossible the free expression of opinion in France through the medium of the press and members of parliament," Bismarck evidently only intended to crack a Ber-

* Borussia: old name for Prussia, frequently used in an ironical sense to indicate the feudal landlord nature of Prussia.

lin joke. If you wish to become acquainted with "true" French opinion, please apply to Herr Stieber, the editor of the Versailles *Moniteur*, and the notorious Prussian police spy! . . .

At Bismarck's express command, Herr Bebel and Liebknecht have been arrested, on a charge of high treason, simply because they dared to do their duty as German members of parliament, *i.e.*, to protest in the Reichstag against the annexation of Alsace and Lorraine, vote against new war credits, express their sympathies with the French Republic, and denounce the attempt to convert Germany into a Prussian barracks. For expressing similar opinions the members of the Brunswick Committee of the Social-Democratic Party have, since the beginning of last September, been treated like galley-slaves, and are still undergoing a ludicrous prosecution for high treason. The same fate has befallen numerous workmen who circulated the Brunswick Manifesto. On similar pretexts, Herr Hepner, the sub-editor of Leipzig *Volksstaat*, had been charged with high treason. The few independent German journals existing outside Prussia are prohibited in the Hohenzollern domains. German workmen's meetings in favour of an honourable peace with France are daily dispersed by the police. According to the official Prussian doctrine, as naively laid down by General Vogel von Falkenstein, every German attempting to counteract the aims of the Prussian military command in France is guilty of high treason. If M. Gambetta and his confrères were, like the Hohenzollerns, compelled to suppress public opinion by force, they would only have to apply the Prussian method and on the plea of war, proclaim throughout France a state of siege. The only French soldiers on German soil rot in Prussian jails. Nevertheless, the Prussian government feels itself bound rigorously to maintain the state of siege, that is to say, the crudest and most revolting form of military despotism, the suspension of all law. The soil of France is infested by almost a million German invaders. Yet the French government can safely dispense with the Prussian methods of "rendering possible the free expression of opinion." Compare the one picture with the other! Germany, however, has proved too narrow a field for Bismarck's all-absorbing passion for the free expression of opinion. When the Luxemburgers gave vent to their sympathies with France, Bismarck made this expression of sentiment one of his pretexts for renouncing the London neutrality treaty. When the Belgian press committed a similar sin, the Prussian ambassador at Brussels, Herr von Balan, invited the Belgian ministry to put down not only all anti-Prussian newspaper articles, but even the printing of reports calculated to encourage the French in their war of liberty. A very modest request this, indeed, to suspend the Belgian constitution *"pour le roi de Prusse."* * No sooner had some Stockholm papers indulged in some mild jokes at the notorious "piety" of Wilhelm *Annexander*,** than Bismarck came down on the Swedish cabinet with grim missives. Even under the meridian of St. Petersburg he contrived to espy too licentious a press. At his humble supplication, the editors of the principal Petersburg papers

* For the King of Prussia. A play on words, for the expression, which can here be taken literally, is also used in the sense of "in vain, for nothing."

** The Annexer. A play on words. A combination of Annexer and Alexander.

were summoned before the Censor-in-Chief, who bade them refrain from all critical observations concerning the faithful Borussian vassal of the tsar. One of these editors, M. Zagulyaev, was imprudent enough to publish the secret of this warning through the columns of the *Golos*. He was at once pounced upon by the Russian police and bundled off to some remote province. It would be a mistake to believe that these gendarme proceedings are only due to the paroxysms of the war fever. They are, on the contrary, the truly methodical application of the spirit of Prussian law. There exists in point of fact a curious proviso in the Prussian criminal code, by virtue of which any foreigner, domiciled in his own or another foreign country, may be prosecuted for "insult to the Prussian king" and "high treason to Prussia"! France—and her cause is fortunately far from desperate—fights at this moment not only for her own national independence, but for the liberty of Germany and Europe.

I am, Sir, yours respectfully,

KARL MARX.

London, January 16.

London, April 12, 1871.

Dear Kugelmann,

Your "doctor's orders" were effective in so far as I consulted my Dr. Matheson and have for the present put myself under his treatment. He says, however, that my lungs are in excellent condition and the coughing is connected with bronchitis, etc. Ditto, it may affect the liver.

Yesterday we received the by no means reassuring news, that Lafargue (not Laura) is in Paris.*

If you look at the last chapter of my *Eighteenth Brumaire* you will find that I say that the next attempt of the French revolution will be no longer, as before, to transfer the bureaucratic military machine from one hand to another, but to *smash* it, and that is essential for every real people's revolution on the Continent. And this is what our heroic Party comrades, in Paris are attempting. What elasticity, what historical initiative, what a capacity for sacrifice in these Parisians! After six months of hunger and ruin, caused rather by internal treachery than by the external enemy, they rise, beneath Prussian bayonets, as if there had never been a war between France and Germany and the enemy were not at the gates of Paris. History has no like example of a like greatness. If they are defeated only their "good nature" will be to blame. They should have marched at once on Versailles, after first Vincy and then the reactionary section of the Paris National Guard had themselves retreated. The right moment was missed because of conscientious scruples. They did not want to *start the civil war*, as if that mischievous *abortion* Thiers had not already started the civil war with his attempt to disarm Paris. Second mistake: The Central Committee surrendered its power too soon, to make way for the Commune. Again from a too "honourable" scrupulosity! However that may be, the present rising in Paris—even if it be crushed by the wolves, swine and vile curs of the old society—is the most glorious deed of our Party since the June insurrection in Paris. Compare these Parisians, storming heaven, with the slaves to

---

* Lafargue had come to Paris from Bordeaux, where he was then living, to obtain from the Commune full powers to organise an armed uprising in Bordeaux.

heaven of the German-Prussian Holy Roman Empire, with its posthumous masquerades reeking of the barracks, the Church, cabbage-junkerdom and above all, of the philistine.

À propos. In the *official publication* of the list of those receiving direct subsidies from Louis Bonaparte's treasury there is a note, that Vogt received 40,000 francs in August 1859. I have informed Liebknecht of the *fait,** for further use.

You can send me the Haxthausen, because *recently* I have received various pamphlets, etc., undamaged, not only from Germany, but even from Petersburg.

Thanks for the newspapers you send me (I would ask you for more, as I want to write something about Germany, the Reichstag, etc.).

Best greetings to the Lady Countess and Fränzchen.

Yours,

K. M.

* Fact.

April 17, 1871.

Dear Kugelmann,

Your letter arrived all right. At the moment I have my hands full. So only a few words. How you can compare petty-bourgeois demonstrations *à la* 13 June 1849, etc., with the present struggle in Paris is quite incomprehensible to me.*

World history would indeed be very easy to make, if the struggle were taken up only on condition of infallibly favourable chances. It would, on the other hand, be of a very mystical nature, if "accidents" played no part. These accidents themselves fall naturally into the general course of development and are compensated again by other accidents. But acceleration and delay are very dependent upon such "accidents," which include the "accident" of the character of those who at first stand at the head of the movement.

The decisive, unfavourable "accident" this time is by no means to be found in the general conditions of French society, but in the presence of the Prussians in France and their position right before Paris. Of this the Parisians were well aware. But of this, the bourgeois *canaille* of Versailles were also well aware. Precisely for that reason they presented the Parisians with the alternative of taking up the fight or succumbing without a struggle. In the latter case, the demoralisation of the working class would have been a far greater misfortune than the fall of any number of "leaders." The struggle of the working class against the capitalist class and its state has entered upon a new phase with the struggle in Paris. Whatever the immediate results may be, a new point of departure of world-historic importance has been gained.

Adio.

K. M.

---

* June 13, 1849, the "Mountain"—the extreme Left wing of the National Assembly—organised a demonstration in Paris to protest against the violent suppression of the Roman Republic by French troops. The demonstration was easily broken up, and indicated the bankruptcy of the petty-bourgeois democrats in France.

London, June 18, 1871.

Dear Kugelmann,

You must forgive my silence, even now I have only time to write a few lines. You know that throughout the period of the last Paris revolution I was denounced continuously as the *grand chef de l'Internationale* by the Versailles papers (Stieber collaborating) and par *répercussion** by the press here in England.

And now the *Address*, which you will have received.** It is making the devil of a noise and I have the honour to be at this moment the best calumniated and the most menaced man of London. That really does one good after a tedious twenty years' idyll in my den. The government paper—the *Observer*—threatens me with a legal prosecution. *Qu'ils osent! Je me moque bien de ces canailles là!* *** I am enclosing a cutting from the *Eastern Post*, because it has our answer to Jules Favre's circular. It appeared originally in the *Times* of June 13. That honourable paper received a severe reprimand from Mr. Bob Lowe (Chancellor of the Exchequer and member of the Supervisory Committee of the *Times*) for this indiscretion.

My best thanks for the Reuters and my best compliments to Madame la Comtesse *et ma chère* Fränzchen.

K. M.

[The enclosure reads as follows:]

International Workingmen's Association.

To the Editor of the *Eastern Post*!

Sir,

On June 6, 1871, M. Jules Favre issued a circular to all the European powers, calling upon them to hunt down the International Workingmen's Association. A few remarks will suffice to characterise that document.

In the very preamble to our Statutes it is stated that the International was founded on September 28, 1864, at a Public Meeting held at St. Martin's Hall, Long Acre, London. For purposes of his own Jules Favre put down the date of its origin as prior to 1862.

In order to expound our principles, he professes to quote from a leaflet of the International's of March 25, 1869. And from what does he quote? From the leaflet of a society that is not the International. To this sort of manœuvre he already had recourse when, still a comparatively young lawyer, he had to defend the *National*, a newspaper which was being sued for libel by Cabet. On this occasion he pretended to read extracts from Cabet's

* By repercussion.
** The Civil War in France, Address of the General Council of the First International.
*** Let them dare! I laugh at these scoundrels!

pamphlets while reading interpolations of his own—a trick that was exposed while the court was sitting and that, but for the indulgence of Cabet, would have been punished by Jules Favre's expulsion from the Paris bar. Of all the documents quoted by him as documents of the International, not one is the work of the International. He says, for example: "The Alliance declares itself atheist, says the General Council, which established itself in London in July 1869." The General Council never issued such a document. On the contrary, it published a document which annulled the original statutes of the Alliance—*L'Alliance de la Démocratie Socialiste* of Geneva—quoted by Jules Favre.

Throughout his circular, which pretends in part also to be directed against the Empire, Jules Favre but repeats against the International the police inventions brought forward by the public prosecutors of the Empire, which broke down miserably even before the law courts of that Empire.

It is known that in its two Addresses (of July and September last) on the late war the General Council of the International denounced the Prussian plans of conquest directed against France. Later on Mr. Reitlinger, Jules Favre's private secretary, applied, though of course in vain, to some members of the General Council with the object of getting the Council to stage a demonstration against Bismarck and in favour of the Government of National Defence; they were expressly requested not to mention the Republic. The preparations for a demonstration in connection with the expected arrival of Jules Favre in London were made—certainly with the best of intentions—in spite of the General Council, which in its address of September 9 had distinctly forewarned the Paris workmen against Jules Favre and his colleagues.

What would Jules Favre say if, in its turn, the International were to send a circular on Jules Favre to all the Cabinets of Europe, drawing their particular attention to the documents published in Paris by the late Millière?

I am, Sir, your obedient servant,

JOHN HALES.*
Secretary of the General Council of the
International Workingmen's Association.
256 High Holborn, W. C., June 12th.

---

* Although signed by Hales, this answer of the General Council was actually written by Marx.

July 27, 1871.

Dear Kugelmann,

Be so good as to send the enclosed note at once to Liebknecht.

I find your silence very strange. I cannot think that the various packages of printed matter have all failed to reach you.

On the other hand it would be very foolish, if you wanted to punish me in this way for not writing—on the old principle of an eye for an eye, a tooth for a tooth. Remember, *mon cher*, that if the day had 48 hours, in the last few months I would still not have finished my day's work.

The work for the International is immense, and in addition London is overrun with refugees, whom we have to look after. Moreover, I am overrun by other people—newspaper men and others of every description—who want to see the "monster" with their own eyes.

Up till now it has been thought that the growth of the Christian myths during the Roman Empire was possible only because printing was not yet invented. Precisely the contrary. The daily press and the telegraph, which in a moment spreads inventions over the whole earth, fabricate more myths (and the bourgeois cattle believe and enlarge upon them) in one day than could have formerly been done in a century.

My daughters have been for some months in the Pyrenees. Jennychen, who was still suffering from the after effects of pleurisy, is, she writes me, getting visibly better.

Best thanks for your Germanic despatches.

I hope that you, as well as your dear wife and Fränzchen— whom I ask you to greet cordially—are well.

A propos! You were probably astonished to see that I made references to a duel in my missive to the *"Pall Mall."* The matter was quite simple. Had I not given the editor this excuse for making a few cheap jokes, he would simply have suppressed the whole letter. As it was he fell into the trap and achieved my real purpose—he published word for word the accusations against Jules Favre and Co. contained in the Address.

Salut.

Yours,

K. M.

November 9, 1871.

Dear Kugelmann,

I still have my hands so overfull with work that I can only write you these few lines.

Document received. It is a worthy imitation of the Viennese model, which was later set aside by the Vienna *cour de cassation.**

Enclosed one French and one English copy of the Resolutions.

Best greetings to Madame la Comtesse and Fränzchen.

Yours,

K. M.

---

* Court of Cassation.

July 9, 1872.

Dear Kugelmann,

My best thanks for the gift of £15 for Jennychen. I have worked myself so hard that today (in two hours) I am leaving London with Engels for four or five days, and going to the sea (Ramsgate). From the date of my return until September 2 (the International Congress at the Hague) I shall have my hands more than full, but from then on I shall again be more free. But this freedom will only begin in the middle of September, because I shall myself go to the Hague.

Perhaps we could see each other later (that is, you could see me, for I would not be safe in Germany).

Adio.

Yours,

KARL MARX.

As soon as the first instalments (German or French) are out, you will of course receive them.* *I am highly dissatisfied with Meissner.* He has led me by the nose—first overworked me due to the sudden and unexpected haste with which he announced the second edition (end of November 1871); then lost months and let the best time slip by. He is a wretched little philistine.

To punish Meissner it would be good if *you were to write him,* on the pretext of wanting to know when the "first" instalment will finally appear. You can then remark, quite in passing, that from my last letters it seemed to you that I am very embittered against Meissner and very dissatisfied with him; what is the reason for that? It is not my usual manner! The fellow has really annoyed me very much by his "if you don't come today, come tomorrow" manner.

---

* The instalments of the second German and first French edition of *Capital.*

July 23, 1872.

Dear Kugelmann,

If nothing happens in between, I shall be at the Hague on 2 September and shall be very glad to see you there. I had already sent you the *Scissions*,* etc., but it seems to have been confiscated. I am therefore enclosing a copy in this letter. You must excuse me for not writing more today. I have to send proofs to Paris and am in general overburdened with business.

Yours,

K. M.

Les prétendues Scissions dans l'Internationale (*The Alleged Scissions in the International*), a pamphlet written by Marx (in French) for the General Council against the Bakunists in the International.

July 29, 1872.

Dear Kugelmann,

At the International Congress (Hague, opening September 2), it will be a matter of life or death for the International; and, before I retire I want at least to protect it from disintegrating elements. Germany must therefore have as many representatives as possible. Since you are in any case coming, write to Hepner that I ask him to get you a delegate's mandate.

Yours,

KARL MARX.

August 26, 1872.

Dear Kugelmann,

At the Hague the delegates will wear blue bands so that the people who come to meet them will recognise them.

In case of accidents:

Private address: Bruno Liebers, 148 Jacob-Catsstraat. *Public Congress Hall:* Concordia, Lombardstraat.

In great haste,

Yours,

K. M.

London, January 19, 1874.

Dear Wenceslas,

Engels gave your letter to me. Hence these few lines. After my return a carbuncle broke out on the right cheek, which was operated on; then it had several smaller successors and I think that at the present moment I am suffering from the *last* of them.

For the rest, don't worry at all about newspaper gossip; *still less answer it.* I myself allow the English papers to announce my death from time to time, without giving a sign of life. Nothing annoys me more than to appear to be supplying the public with reports of my state of health through my friends (*you are the greatest sinner in this respect*). I don't give a farthing for the public, and, if my occasional illness is exaggerated, it at least has this advantage, that it keeps away all sorts of requests (theoretical and otherwise) from unknown people in every corner of the earth.

My best thanks for the kind words from the lady countess and Fränzchen.

I am very glad to receive the *Frankfurter Zeitung* and find many interesting things in it.

The relative victory of the ultramontanes * and social-democrats in the elections serves Mr. Bismarck and his middle class tail right. More another time.

Yours,

K. M.

À propos: On the advice of my friend, Dr. Gumpert (Manchester), I now use quicksilver ointment at the first trace of carbuncle irritation and find that it works quite specifically.

What has happened to your friend, "Dr. Freund," of Breslau, who in your opinion was so promising? It seems, *après tout, que c'est un fruit sec.***

---

* Militant Catholics, referring here to the Catholic Centre Party. In the Reichstag elections of 1874, the Centre achieved a great victory, receiving 91 mandates (1,500,000 votes) in place of the 63 received in 1871. The Social-Democrats obtained 351,670 votes (9 mandates) compared with 101,927 in 1874.

** After all, that this is a dry fruit.

Dear Kugelmann,   May 18, 1874.

I have received everything: your letters (including some friendly notes from your dear wife and Fränzchen), the "Meyer" (police-socialist, *faiseur*,** literary scribbler), the cuttings from the *Frankfurter*, etc., and finally a letter from Madame Tenge.

I am very grateful for your, your family's and Madame Tenge's friendly interest in my progress. But you do me an injustice if you ascribe my failure to write to any other cause than an uncertain state of health, which continually interrupts my work, then goads me on to make up for the time lost by neglecting all other duties (letters included), and finally puts a man out of humour and makes him disinclined for activity.

After my return from Harrogate I had an attack of carbuncles, then my headaches returned, insomnia, etc., so that I had to spend from the middle of April to May 5 at Ramsgate (seaside). Since then I have been feeling much better, but am far from being quite well. My specialist (Dr. Gumpert of Manchester) insists upon my going to Karlsbad and would like to make me travel there as soon as possible, but I must finally complete the French translation which has come to a full stop, and, apart from that, I should much prefer it if I could meet you there.

In the meantime, while I was unable to write, I worked through a lot of important new material for the second volume. But I cannot start on its final working out until the French edition is completed and my health fully restored.

So I have by no means yet decided how I shall spend the summer. The progress of the German labour movement (ditto in Austria) is wholly satisfactory. In France the absence of a theoretical foundation and of practical common sense is very evident. In England at the moment only the rural labour movement shows any advance; the industrial workers have first of all to get rid of their present leaders. When I denounced them at the Hague Congress I knew that I was letting myself in for unpopularity, slander, etc., but such consequences have always been a matter of indifference to me. Here and there people are beginning to see that in making that denunciation I was only doing my duty.

* Rudolph Meyer.
** Mountebank.

In the United States our Party has to fight against great difficulties, partly economic, partly political, but it is making headway. The greatest obstacle there is the professional politicians, who immediately try to falsify every new movement and change it into a new "company-promoting business."

Notwithstanding all diplomatic moves, a new war is inevitable *au peu plus tôt, au peu plus tard,** and before the ending of this there will hardly be violent popular movements anywhere, or, at the most, they will remain local and unimportant.

The visit of the Russian emperor is giving the London police a great deal to do and the government here will be glad to get rid of the man as soon as possible. As a precautionary measure they requisitioned forty police (mouchards), with the notorious police commissioner Plocke at their head (Ali Baba and the forty thieves), from the French Government, to watch the Poles and Russians here (during the tsar's stay). The so-called amnesty petition of the London Poles is the work of the Russian embassy; in answer to it the Poles here issued an appeal, written and signed by Wroblewski, which is addressed to the English and which has been distributed in large numbers at the Sunday meetings in Hyde Park. The English press (with very few exceptions) is obsequious—the tsar is after all "our guest"—but for all that the real feeling against Russia is incomparably more hostile than it has been since the Crimean War, and the entry of a Russian princess into the royal family ** has aroused rather than disarmed suspicion. The facts—the arbitrary abrogation of the decisions concerning the Black Sea in the Paris Treaty, the conquests and trickeries in Central Asia, etc., irritate John Bull, and Disraeli has no chance of remaining at the helm for any length of time if he continues Gladstone's unctuous foreign policy.

With my warmest greetings to your dear family and Madame Tenge.

Yours,

K. M.

* Sooner or later.
** The betrothal of the Grand Duchess Maria to Prince Alfred, Duke of Edinburgh.

June 24, 1874.

Dear Kugelmann,

I have at last decided to go to Karlsbad in the middle of August with my youngest daughter Eleanor (called Tussy). You must therefore see about lodgings and inform me how much it will cost per week. What happens later will depend on circumstances.

My best greetings to the Lady Countess and Fränzchen.

Yours,

K. M.

The Austrian government would be stupid enough to put difficulties in my way; it is therefore advisable to let nobody know anything of the intended journey.

August 4, 1874.

Dear Kugelmann,

About eight days ago I wrote your dear wife a few lines, telling her of the death of my only grandson and the severe illness of my youngest daughter. This was not an isolated but rather an acute outbreak of an illness from which she has long suffered. Eleanor is now up again, much sooner than her doctor (Madame Dr. Anderson-Garrett) had hoped. She is able to travel, though of course still delicate. Madame Anderson thinks the Karlsbad waters will help considerably to restore her health, just as Dr. Gumpert ordered rather than recommended me to go there. It is difficult for me to leave Jenny now (I mean in about two weeks). I am in this respect less stoical than in others and family afflictions always hit me hard. The more one lives, as I do, almost cut off from the outside world, the more one is caught in the emotional life of one's own circle.

You must send me your exact Karlsbad address and, in particular, make my excuses to your wife and Fränzchen for not answering their friendly and affectionate letters.

Yours,

K. M.

August 10, 1874.

Dear Kugelmann,

I cannot start from here before the 15th August (Saturday) and shall take about four days to get to our destination, since Tussy must not exert herself too much.

Salut.

Yours,

K. M.

BIOGRAPHICAL INDEX

BIOGRAPHICAL INDEX

BAKUNIN, M. A. (1814-71)—Revolutionary anarchist. Head of the anarchist opposition against Marx in the First International. Especially after the defeat of the Paris Commune, he objectively assisted the reaction.

BASTIAT, Frederic (1801-50)—French vulgar economist of the free-trade school.

BAUER, Bruno (1809-82)—German philosopher and publicist. At first a member of the group of radical young Hegelians, later joined the conservatives. Did work of scientific value in regard to the history of early Christianity.

BEBEL, August (1840-1913)—One of the founders and leaders of the German Social-Democratic Party and of the Second International.

BECKER, Bernhard (Committed suicide in 1882)—German publicist and historian. A follower of Lassalle, after whose death he became president of the General Association of German Workers (*Allgemeiner Deutscher Arbeiterverein*). Later he joined the Social-Democratic Labour Party founded by Bebel and Liebknecht (the Eisenachers).

BECKER, Johann Phillip (1800-86)—Member of the First International and an active supporter of Marx in the latter's struggle against Bakunin. Editor of *Der Vorbote*, the German organ of the First International, published in Geneva.

BEESLY, Edward Spencer (1831-1915)—Historian and leader of the English followers of Comte. A supporter of social reforms and pacifism. Presided at the meeting at which the First International was founded and remained on friendly terms with Marx.

BENEDEK, Ludwig (1804-81)—Austrian general, took part in the Austro-Prussian war of 1866.

BLANQUI, Auguste (1805-81)—French revolutionary. An active supporter of the revolutionary movement in France from 1830 on. Spent nearly thirty-seven years of his life in prison.

BLIND, Karl (1826-1907)—German publicist and petty-bourgeois democrat. Later supported Bismarck.

BÖHM, Jakob (1575-1624)—German mystical philosopher, a cobbler by trade.

BÖRKHEIM, Sigismund (1825-85)—German merchant and publicist who took an active part in the 1848 Revolution. Fled to Switzerland and later settled in London, where in the 'sixties he became a close friend of Marx and Engels.

BRACKE, Wilhelm (1842-80)—Active member of the German Social-Democratic movement. At first a Lassallean, later an Eisenacher. Stood close to Marx.

BRENTANO, Lujo (1844-1931)—German economist of the "professorial socialist" school.

BUCHER, Lothar (1817-92)—German publicist and politician. A radical democrat in 1848. In the 'sixties he entered Bismarck's service.

BÜCHNER, Ludwig (1824-99)—German vulgar materialist scientist.

BÜRGERS, Heinrich (1820-78)—One of the editors of the *Neue Rheinische Zeitung*; active member of the Communist League. In 1852, in the Communist trial at Cologne, was sentenced to six years' imprisonment in a fortress. After his liberation he joined the progressive democrats.

CABANIS, Pierre (1757-1808)—French philosopher and doctor. An inconsistent materialist.

CABET, Etienne (1788-1856)—French lawyer and publicist. An utopian communist and author of the *Voyage en Icarie*(1840)in which he sketched his plan of a communist society.

CAREY, Henry (1793-1879)—American economist.

CASSAGNAC, Adolph (1806-80)—French writer. First an Orleanist, later Bonapartist.

CAVAIGNAC, L. (1802-57)—French general who organised the massacre of the Parisian workers in June 1848.

COMTE, August (1798-1857)—French philosopher and leader of the positivist school. A supporter of social reform.

CONTZEN, Heinrich—German vulgar economist.

DELESCLUZE, Louis Charles (1809-71)—Took part in the Revolution of 1848 in France and in the Paris Commune of 1871. Fell fighting on the barricades, May 28, 1871.

DIETZGEN, Joseph (1828-88)—German socialist and self-educated philosopher; leather tanner by trade. A dialectical materialist although an inconsistent one. Later lived in the U.S.A. where he took part in the socialist movement.

DOLFUS, Jean (1808-87)—Alsatian manufacturer and free-trader. Became known on account of the cheap dwellings he caused to be built for his workers, with a view to keeping them in bondage.

DUCHINSKI, Francisque (1817-80)—Polish patriot, historian and publicist. Author of the theory of the Mongolian origin of the Great Russians.

DÜHRING, Eugen (1833-1922)—German positivist philosopher, Engels' book *Anti-Dühring* was devoted to combating his views which had great influence among many German socialists at the end of the 'seventies.

ECCARIUS, George (1818-89)—German socialist, living in London. Secretary of the General Council of the First International and active participant in the London trade union movement.

FALKENSTEIN, Vogel von (1797-1898)—Prussian general who ordered the arrest and imprisonment in chains of the members of the Braunschweig Committee of the Social-Democratic Party because of their protest against the annexation of Alsace-Lorraine.

FALLOUX, Frederic (1811-66)—French politician; responsible for the dissolution of the national workshops and the massacres of June 1848 in Paris. Author of a reactionary plan of national education.

FAUCHER, Julius (1802-78)—German economist of the free-trade school. For a time Cobden's personal secretary.

FAVRE, Jules (1809-80)—French politician. Member of the Government of "National Defence" in 1870-71. One of the bitterest enemies of the Commune.

FIELDEN, John (1784-1849)—Economist, manufacturer and advocate of labour legislation. Author of the book *The Curse of the Factory System.* Came out against child labour in England.

FOURIER, Charles (1772-1837)—French utopian socialist; a brilliant critic of capitalist society.

FREILIGRATH, Ferdinand (1810-76)—German revolutionary poet. In 1848-49 termed the "trumpet of the revolution." A contributor to the *Neue Rheinische Zeitung.* A friend of Marx up to the 'fifties, after which he joined the petty-bourgeois democrats in London.

FRIBOURG, E. S.—A French engraver; a Proudhonist. Took part in the First International.

FRIEDRICH KARL (1828-85)—Prussian Prince and general.

GAMBETTA, Leon (1838-82)—Leader of the French republican party during the Second Empire and organiser of national defence during the Franco-Prussian war.

GARIBALDI, Giuseppe (1807-82)—Leader of the Italian national liberation movement in 1848-70.

GNEISENAU, August (1760-1831)—Prussian general active in the wars against Napoleon I.

GÖGG—Wife of a South German petty-bourgeois democrat and pacifist.

GORCHAKOV, Prince A. (1793-1883)—Russian Minister for Foreign Affairs under Alexander II.

GUILLAUME, James (1844-1916)—Leader of the Swiss and French anarchists and Bakunin's adherent in the struggle against Marx in the First International.

GUIZOT, François (1787-1874)—French statesman and historian; Prime Minister, 1840-48.

GUMPERT (Died 1895)—German doctor in Manchester and friend of Marx and Engels.

HALES, John—Secretary to the General Council of the First International in 1871 and leader of the English secessionists after the Hague Congress of 1872.

HATZFELD, Countess Sophie von (1806-81)—Friend of Lassalle, who conducted her divorce case 1848-54. After his death she broke with the Lassallean General Association of German Workers.

HAXTHAUSEN, August von (1792-1867)—German economist. In his book: *On the Agrarian Structure of Russia,* he was the first to acquaint Western Europe with the Russian village commune.

HELD, Adolf (1844-80)—German economist and "professorial socialist."

HEPNER, Adolf (1846-1923)—A German Social-Democrat, co-editor of *Volksstaat.* On trial together with Liebknecht and Bebel in 1872 for high treason, but was acquitted.

HERZEN, A. I. (1812-70)—Famous Russian politician and writer. One of the founders of the *Narodnik* movement and Russian liberalism. Lived in emigration, chiefly in London and Geneva.

HIRSCH, Karl (1841-1900)—German publicist and Lassallean. Later joined Liebknecht and Bebel with whom he worked on the *Volksstaat.* In the 'sixties and 'seventies he stood close to Marx.

HOFSTETTEN, Johann Baptist von (?-1857)—Formerly a Prussian officer, then co-editor of the Lassallean organ *Neuer Sozialdemokrat.* (See note p. 56.)

JAKOBI, Abraham (1832-1900)—German doctor and in his youth an active member of the Communist League at Cologne. Sentenced in the

Cologne trial of 1852; after serving his sentence emigrated to America, and left the labour movement.

JACOBY, Johann (1805-77)—German radical. "One of the very rare German bourgeois democrats who, after the lessons of 1870-71, went over not to chauvinism or German liberalism but to socialism." (Lenin.)

JONES, Ernest (1819-69)—Chartist, lawyer and poet. Editor of the *People's Paper* and *Notes to the People*, to both of which Marx contributed. At times stood close to Marx and Engels.

JUNG, Hermann (1830-1901)—German watchmaker, active in the First International, secretary of the Swiss section of the General Council.

KAUB, C.—German emigrant in Paris. In the 'fifties and 'sixties, friendly to Marx.

KINKEL, Gottfried (1815-82)—German publicist and writer; petty-bourgeois democrat. Later went over to Bismarck.

KERTBENY, Charles—Hungarian writer, active in the Revolution of 1848-49. While in emigration he wrote for the German press.

KOSSUTH, Louis (1802-92)—Leader of the Hungarian Revolutionary Government of 1848-49 and of the Hungarian national struggle against Austria.

LAFARGUE, Paul (1842-1911)—A pupil of Marx who married Marx's daughter, Laura. An active member of the First International. One of the leaders of the French Workers' Party.

LANGE, Friedrich Albert (1828-75)—German petty-bourgeois democrat, philosopher; follower of Kant.

LASSALLE, Ferdinand (1825-64)—German politician and writer who played an important role in the German labour movement, in which he was the founder of reformism. (See also note on p. 24.)

LAW, Henrietta—English authoress. Active in the Left wing of the anti-religious movement.

LEDRU-ROLLIN (1807-74)—French politician, petty-bourgeois democrat.

LESSING, Gotthold Ephraim (1729-81)—German writer, leader of the Enlightenment of the eighteenth century.

LIEBKNECHT, Wilhelm (1826-1900)—One of the most prominent leaders of German Social-Democracy and of the international labour movement from the 'seventies to the 'nineties. Father of Karl Liebknecht.

LOCHNER, Georg (born about 1826)—German working man, emigrant in London. Member of the Communist League and later of the General Council of the First International.

LOWE, Robert (Viscount Sherbrooke) (1811-92)—Liberal statesman and member of Palmerston's cabinet.

MALTHUS, Robert (1766-1834)—English economist and parson. Author of the reactionary theory of over-population.

MARIE, Alexander Pierre (1791-1870)—Bourgeois republican, member of the French Provisional Government of 1848, organiser of the national workshops. Supported the suppression of the workers' insurrection of June.

MARR, Wilhelm (1819-1904)—German publicist. In the 'forties an active supporter of the revolutionary movement of the German-Swiss artisans. After 1870 a fanatical anti-Semite.

MARTIN, Henri (1810-83)—French historian, Republican Nationalist.

MARX, Eleanor (Tussy) (1856-98)—Youngest daughter of Karl Marx. Took an active part in the English workers' movement.

MARX, Jenny (1844-82)—Eldest daughter of Karl Marx for whom she did a great deal of work as secretary. Under the pseudonym of J. Williams she contributed a series of articles to the *Marseillaise* (Paris) in support of the Fenian movement.

MARX, Laura (1846-1911)—Marx's second daughter and wife of Paul Lafargue.

MENDELSSOHN, Moses (1729-86)—German philosopher.

MEYER, Rudolph (1839-99)—German conservative publicist. Opposed Bismarck from the Right and was therefore persecuted. Emigrated abroad. Author of the book, *The Emancipation Struggle of the Fourth Estate* (1872-74). One of the founders of the Christian Socialist Party in Austria.

MEYER, Siegfried (1840-72)—German socialist and devoted adherent of Marx. Emigrated to America in 1866 and helped to organise the German workers there in the First International.

MILLIÈRE, J. B. (1817-71)—French revolutionary and writer. A Proudhonist. Took part in the Paris Commune. Shot by the Versaillese.

MIQUEL, Johannes (1828-1901)—German statesman; in the early 'fifties a supporter of Marx and active member of the Communist League. In the 'sixties he joined the National Liberals. Later, Prussian Minister of Finance.

MIRABEAU, Honoré Gabriel (1749-91)—Leader of the French Revolution in its first period; advocate of constitutional monarchy and protagonist of the financial aristocracy.

MOHL, Moritz (1802-88)—German vulgar economist.

MOILIN, Tony (1832-71)—French doctor and writer on medical subjects; he also wrote a book on the labour question. Active supporter of the Commune and doctor for the Commune army; was captured and shot by the Versaillese.

MÖSER, Justus von (1720-84)—German publicist and historian, burgomaster of Osnabrück.

ODGER, George (1820-77)—Trade union leader; a shoemaker by trade; member of the London Trade Council and the General Council of the International, from which he resigned after the publication of the *Civil War in France.* Later joined the Liberals.

OWEN, Robert (1771-1858)—The most prominent English utopian socialist.

PALMERSTON, Henry Temple, Viscount (1784-1865)—British statesman and diplomat against whom Marx wrote a series of articles in the *New York Tribune,* later published in England as *Political Flysheets.*

PELLETAN, Eugene (1813-84)—Radical French journalist, member of the Government of National Defence in 1870 and of the Senate in the Third Republic.

PERRON, Charles—Geneva workman, one of the founders of the Bakuninist "Alliance."

PERRET—A prominent Bakuninist in Geneva, editor of *Égalité* (*Equality*).

PERTZ, Georg (1795-1876)—German historian.

POTTER, George (1832-93)—English working class leader, active in the trade union movement of the 'fifties and 'sixties. Parliamentary candidate in 1868. Editor of the *Beehive.* Later joined the Liberals.

PROUDHON, Pierre Joseph (1809-65)—Classical representative of petty-bourgeois socialism. The theoretician of peaceful anarchism. To his

Philosophy of Poverty (1846) Marx replied with the *Poverty of Philosophy* (1847).

PYAT, Felix (1810-89)—French petty-bourgeois revolutionary. Took part in the Revolution of 1848 and was a member of the Committee of Public Safety in the Paris Commune.

QUETELET, Lambert Adolphe (1796-1874)—Eminent Belgian statistician and founder of modern social statistics.

RASCH, Gustav (?-1878)—German publicist and democrat.

RAU, Karl Heinrich (1792-1870)—German economist, leader of the economic school combining mercantilism and free-trade.

REICH, Edward (1836-1904)—Doctor, anthropologist and writer on religion, crime, etc.

REITLINGER—Personal secretary of Jules Favre.

REUTER, Fritz (1810-74) Prominent German novelist. Sentenced to death in 1833 for his part in the student movement, reprieved and amnestied in 1840.

RICARDO, David (1772-1823)—The most eminent representative of the classical school of political economy in England.

ROSSA, O'Donovan Jeremy (1831-?)—Irish nationalist and revolutionary, frequently arrested by the British government; emigrated to America in 1870.

RÜGE, Arnold (1812-80)—Radical German publicist and politician well known as a Left Hegelian. Together with Marx published the *Deutsch-Französischer Jahrbücher* in Paris in 1846. Fled to London after the Revolution of 1848, in which he took part. Remained a petty-bourgeois democrat until the 'seventies when he went over to the side of Bismarck.

SCHEDO-FERROTI (pseudonym of Baron F. L. Firks) (1812-72)—Russian government official in the Ministry of Finance.

SCHILY, Viktor (1810-75)—Lawyer at Trier; took an active part in the Baden rising of 1849; a close friend of Marx and Engels. Emigrated to Paris, where he consistently advocated the views of Marx in the French sections of the International. Was of great service to Marx in exposing K. Vogt.

SCHNAKE, Friedrich—German journalist in the 'forties; a representative of "true socialism"; in the 'sixties a progressive democrat. (See note on p. 68.)

SCHRAMM, Konrad (1822-58)—Member of the Communist League and participant in the Revolution of 1848. Friend of Marx and Engels. Lived in emigration in Paris, London and later in the U.S.A.

SCHRAMM, Rudolf (1813-82)—German politician, member of the Prussian National Assembly and president of the Berlin Democratic Club. Emigrated after the 1848 Revolution and became an opponent of Marx and Engels. On his return to Germany he supported Bismarck and obtained a diplomatic appointment.

SCHULZE-DELITZSCH, Hermann (1803-83)—German economist and politician; a democrat. An advocate of the co-operative movement with the aim of subordinating the labour movement to the policy of the democrats.

SCHWEITZER, Johann Baptist (1833-75)—German working class leader; friend of Lassalle. After the death of Lassalle, leader of the Lassalleans until 1871.

SIEBEL, Karl (1836-68)—Radical poet and distant relation of Engels.

During his stay in England from 1856-60 he became a friend of Marx and contributed to the popularisation of *Capital* in Germany.

SIMON, Jules (1814-96)—French bourgeois republican politician. Member of the Provisional Government in 1870, one of the leaders in the defeat of the Paris Commune.

STEPNEY-COWELL, Fred—Treasurer of the First International, 1869-72.

STIEBER, Wilhelm (1818-82)—Chief of the political department of the Prussian police and organiser of the famous Communist trial at Cologne in 1852.

STROHN, Wilhelm—German merchant; a member of the Communist League and, as an emigrant in England, a friend of Marx and Engels.

STRUVE, Gustav (1805-70)—German radical and one of the leaders of the Baden insurrection of 1848-49. Later emigrated to America where he fought in the Civil War against the southern states.

STUMPF, Paul (1827-1913)—Member of the Communist League and of the First International. Friend of Marx and Engels.

SZEMERE, Bartholomew (1812-69)—One of the leaders of the Hungarian Revolution of 1848-49. In the 'fifties while in emigration he headed the Left opposition against Kossuth. In this period Marx supported him.

TÈNOT, Eugene (1839-90)—French radical republican and writer.

THIERS, Louis Adolph (1797-1877)—French statesman and historian. Prime Minister in 1836-40. As leader of the National Assembly in 1871, he was the most ferocious opponent of the Commune and organised the massacres of the Communards in the May days. President of the Republic, 1871-73.

THÜNEN, Johann Heinrich (1783-1850)—German economist. Author of the book, *The Isolated State in Relation to Agriculture.*

TOLAIN, Henri (1828-97)—French working class leader; Proudhonist and one of the founders of the French section of the International; member of the National Assembly in 1871. For his hostile attitude to the Commune he was expelled from the International. Senator under the Third Republic in 1876.

TRIDON, Gustav (1841-71)—French writer and member of the Commune. Together with Blanqui published the newspaper, the *Fatherland in Danger.*

TROCHU, Louis (1815-98)—French general, commander of the Parisian forces in 1870-71. Out of fear of the revolution, he sabotaged the defence of Paris.

URQUHART, David (1805-77)—English diplomat, Turcophile and opponent of Palmerston whom he accused of secret alliance with tsarism.

VERMOREL, Auguste (1841-71)—French publicist and historian. An active member of the Commune, a Proudhonist. He was mortally wounded on the barricades in May 1871.

VIRCHOV, Rudolf (1821-1902)—Famous German medical scientist and petty-bourgeois democrat.

VOGT, Karl (1871-95)—German natural scientist, vulgar materialist and petty-bourgeois democrat. After the Revolution of 1848-49 he lived in Switzerland, an active member of the "League of Peace and Liberty." In his book, *Herr Vogt,* Marx proved that during the Italian war Vogt acted as agent of Napoleon III (in 1870 it was proved by documentary evidence that he was in the pay of Napoleon).

WROBLEWSKI, Valerian (1836-1908)—Emigrant Polish revolutionary; one of the military leaders of the Commune.

WAGNER, Hermann (1815-89)—Reactionary German politician, a close supporter of Bismarck.

WARNEBOLD—Active member of the *National Union* in Hanover.

WEERTH, Georg (1821-56)—Revolutionary German poet; member of the Communist League and intimate friend of Marx and Engels, with whom he worked on the *Neue Rheinische Zeitung* (1848-49). Engels called him "the first poet of the German proletariat."

WINDTHORST, Ludwig (1812-91)—Leader of the Catholic Centre in the German Reichstag. He led the opposition against Bismarck.

WOLFF, Wilhelm (1809-64)—The son of a Silesian serf. A close friend of Marx and Engels. Active in the 1848 Revolution, was associate editor of the *Neue Rheinische Zeitung*. Fled to England after the revolution. Marx dedicated to him the first volume of *Capital*.

ZAGULYAEV, M. A. (1834-1900)—Russian liberal publicist.

In response, Lord Loss picks up his king and crushes it softly between his mangled fingers.

"Two-two," he croaks, and turns to the board on my far left — the final board — the decider.

✠ Lord Loss moves his pieces sluggishly. He plays with sad remoteness, face cast in dull misery, flinching every time I capture one of his pieces, handing the game to me without a real fight.

I feel a bubble of joy rising in my chest — and swiftly move to burst it. If I show any emotion now, he might seize upon it and revive with a flourish. Although it's difficult, I remain detached, moving my pieces instinctively, automatically, not dwelling upon thoughts of victory.

Gradually I rip his defenses to shreds. I check his king and he beats a sad retreat. For a couple of moves he threatens my queen, but then I drag her out of the way and check him again, with a rook. For a second time his king is forced to flee.

A short while later I trap him on the left side of the board. He's caught between my queen, two knights, and a bishop. He starts to move his king. Pauses. Does a double-take. Sighs deeply and slowly tips the king over.

"Checkmate," he intones morosely.

I blink — I hadn't seen it. "Are you sure?" I ask, frowning.

In response he pushes himself away from the table and floats out of his chair, face impassive.

Real time crashes over me. I'm hit by a wave of hot air. Sounds — Bill-E's howls, the snapping of Vein and Artery's teeth, Dervish's grunts. I spin. My uncle's on the floor, furiously wrestling with the demons. Blood everywhere. His left leg cut to ribbons. His right hand chewed off.

"Stop them!" I scream, darting to Dervish's aid.

Artery hears me, turns, and snarls. Spreads his hands wide — morsels of Dervish's flesh caught between his teeth. Rises to meet me.

"Peace, Artery," Lord Loss says, and the demon stops. "Cease, Vein," he commands, and the crocodile-headed monster quits chewing on Dervish's arm and looks questioningly at her master. "I have been beaten. We must respect the rules of the game."

The demons chatter and gibber madly. The flames in Artery's eyes flare and he hisses at his lord, shaking his head negatively. Vein snaps her jaws open and shut, then turns again on Dervish.

"You will obey me," Lord Loss says softly, "or I shall have your heads."

The demons pause. Then Vein clamps her teeth around Dervish's arm. Dervish screams. A blinding red light fills the cellar. I shut my eyes and cover my face with my arms. When I dare look again, Vein's lying in scraps of bloody flesh around my uncle. Artery has backed up to one of the webs and is whimpering fearfully.

Lord Loss floats over to Dervish and studies him blankly as he sits up and sets to work on his injuries, using magic to patch himself back together.

"I won," I remark, carefully approaching my preoccupied uncle, wary of Lord Loss — he might have killed the rebellious Vein, but I still don't trust him.

"So I see," Dervish says, not glancing up from his wounds.

I'm bitterly disappointed by his reaction. I expected cheers and tears, hugging and back-slapping — not this.

"You needn't sound so excited about it," I sniff.

Dervish looks up at me. A thin smile crosses his lips, then vanishes. "I'm delighted, Grubbs," he sighs. "Truly. But this isn't over for me. I have to fight Lord Loss now, and it's a fight I probably won't win. So while I'm ecstatic for you and Billy, I'm a little too worried about myself to celebrate."

"What are you talking about? We won. I beat him. We can . . ."

I stop, recalling the full rules of the challenge. Lord Loss is under oath to cure the person affected by lycanthropy if he loses at chess — but the one who beats him has to travel to the Demonata's universe and fight him there.

"But *I* beat him!" I cry, stooping to catch Dervish's eye. "*I'm* the one who has to go with him and —"

"No," Dervish interrupts. "The player always goes, while the one who fought the familiars remains. But since we swapped roles, we can choose who goes and stays. Isn't that right?" he asks Lord Loss.

Lord Loss nods slightly. "It is an ambiguous point, but I have had enough of the boy. I shall seek him out some other time. As I vowed, he will pay for his humiliation of me, but for now I wish only to wash my hands of him."

"But you're wounded!" I protest. "You're not fit to fight anymore. Let me. I know how to beat him. I can do it. I'll —"

"This isn't a debate," Dervish says gruffly. He grips both my hands in his and squeezes tightly. "You performed brilliantly on the boards, Grubbs, but this is a different matter.

He's far stronger in his own universe than he is here. Leave it to me, OK?"

Tears roll down my cheeks unchecked. "I don't want to lose you," I sob.

"But you must," he says, smiling. "At least for a while." He finishes healing himself and stands, groaning loudly. Turns to Lord Loss. "The cure?"

Lord Loss sneers. "I had not forgotten." He floats across the room to the cage. Bill-E backs away, snarling fitfully, but at a gesture from the demon master he flies across the cage and thrusts his arms through the bars. Lord Loss wraps two of his own arms around Bill-E's and slides the other six through the bars of the cage, encompassing the struggling werewolf. He exerts pressure, until Bill-E goes stiff, then presses his face forward, places his lips over Bill-E's, and exhales heavily, as though giving the kiss of life.

Bill-E's fingers fly out rigidly, then curl up into tight fists. His legs shake fitfully, then go slack. After ten or twelve seconds, Lord Loss breaks contact and releases Bill-E. He floats backwards, coughing and spitting. Bill-E teeters on his feet a moment, then crumples to the floor.

I start towards my brother, concerned. Dervish stops me. "Wait. He'll be OK. There are things I must tell you before we say goodbye." I face my uncle, who speaks quickly. "You know where the forms, credit cards, and contact numbers are. Use them. Act swiftly. Don't be ashamed to ask for help. And don't let the authorities take you away from here. They might interfere when they discover the condition I'm in, seek to separate you from me. Don't let them." His face is grim. "Lord Loss has threatened you — that's serious. He can't harm you in Carcery Vale — as long as you stay out of this cellar — but you're vulnerable elsewhere. In time you'll learn spells to protect yourself — friends of mine will help — but for now you mustn't leave the Vale."

"What can I do to stop them?" I ask.

"Stand up to them. Sic my lawyers — *your* lawyers — on them. Be brave. Prove you're fit to live independently. Don't give them any excuse to take you away. Meera will help — if she recovers — but you'll have to do a lot of it yourself."

Lord Loss has drifted to the edge of the cellar while we've been talking. He's floating in front of a thick bank of webs, gesturing at them with all eight arms, muttering something inhuman. Artery has crept up beside his master and squats sullenly next to him.

As I watch, the webs shimmer, then twist in a clockwise direction, winding and wrapping together. The center of the web pulses outwards a couple of times, then stretches backwards at lightning speed, cutting a path through the layers of webs behind it, creating an impossibly long, rotating funnel from the cellar to some indefinite point beyond.

"Take care of Billy," Dervish says. "He won't remember any of this. It's up to you how much you tell him. I won't advise you one way or the other on that point. If you start to change . . ." He hesitates, then presses on. "Meera and one of my other friends might challenge Lord Loss on your behalf. If you want to make a fight of it, ask Meera, and she can —"

"No," I interrupt softly. "I won't put anybody else through this. It wouldn't be fair. If the curse hits me, I'll abandon myself to it, call in the Lambs. But I won't ask anyone to face Lord Loss for me."

Dervish smiles wanly. "You might lose some of those noble ideals when you get a bit older." His smile softens. "But I hope not."

"It is time, Dervish Grady," Lord Loss says. The spiraling funnel he's created glows redly, the webs revolving rapidly. Artery leaps onto the web at the rim of the funnel. He's sucked into it instantly. Spins around several times, head over heels, then vanishes down the funnel's maw, never to be seen in these parts again — I hope.

"*Must* you go?" I sob, clutching Dervish's hands.

"Yes," he answers simply. "If I refused, he could bring his hordes of familiars through and destroy us all."

"How will I know . . . if you're . . . successful?" I gulp.

"As long as I'm fighting, I'll be an emotionless shell here," he says. "If I lose, that won't change, and you'll never know — I'll simply die of old age. But if I win . . ." He winks. "Don't worry — you'll soon find out!"

Dervish faces Lord Loss and the funnel. Takes a deep breath. Holds it. Lets it out nervously. "Remember, Grubbs," he mutters. "Don't give up on me. No matter how much time passes — even if it's decades — there's always hope."

"I'll look after you," I promise, weeping uncontrollably.

"Your Mom and Dad would have been proud of you tonight," Dervish says. "Gret too."

With that, he turns his back on me and marches to the funnel. Lord Loss bows politely as he approaches, then unfolds all eight of his arms and strikes for Dervish's throat. Dervish ducks swiftly, avoiding the demon master's lunge.

"Uh-uh!" he laughs. "You won't make that quick a finish of me!"

Leaping over the demon, he grabs hold of a thick strand of web, spins around, hollering wildly, then disappears down the funnel, becoming a speck, then nothing.

Lord Loss floats towards the opening. Glances back at me, eyes cold and hateful. "In the past, I've respected those who bested me," he snarls. "But you belittled both the game and me. I will be keeping a close watch on you, Grubitsch Grady, and if you ever —"

"My name's Grubbs," I grunt, cutting him short. I step forward, wiping tears from my face. "Now piss off back to your own world, you motherless scum, and save your threats for those who care."

For a moment it looks like he's going to abandon protocol and rip me to shreds. But then he snarls, whirls away from me, and hurls himself into the funnel of webs. There's a flash. The world turns red, then black. The webs fade. The funnel blinks out of existence. Walls and ceiling slowly return.

It ends.

THE CHANGE

✠   ✠   ✠

WORKING numbly. A quick trip to the house to fetch new candles. Then I sweep debris — broken chess boards and pieces — out of the way. Methodical. Chasing every last splinter and shard. Stacking them neatly against the walls. Need to keep active. Not dwelling on the game or the fight — or Dervish.

His body rematerialized as reality returned. But only his body — not his mind. He stands by the wall to my left, vacant, unresponsive, eyes glazed over.

Bill-E regains consciousness — and humanity — as I'm coming towards the end of my big cleanup. "Where am I?" he mutters. "What's happening?" He stands shakily and stares at the bars of the cage. His voice rises fearfully. "What am I doing here? Where's Dervish? What's —"

"It's OK," I shush him, fetching the key and unlocking the door. "Dervish is over by that wall. There's no need to be afraid."

Bill-E stumbles out of the cage and glances nervously at

the eerily motionless man in the candle-lit shadows. "What's the story?" he asks. "The last thing I remember is following Dervish — then nothing."

I haven't thought about what I'm going to tell Bill-E. So I say the first thing that comes into my head.

"We were right — Dervish was a werewolf. He knocked you out and brought you here. I tracked him and fought with him. He recovered. He was grief-stricken when he realized what he'd done — the change had never affected him this way before. He gave me a book with a spell in it and told me to cast it."

"What sort of a spell?" Bill-E asks, edging closer to Dervish.

"A calming spell," I improvize. "He'd been saving it for an emergency. It stops him from turning into a werewolf — but it also robs him of his personality. He's like a zombie now. He can't speak or respond. I don't know how long he'll stay that way — maybe forever. But if he recovers, he'll be safe. He won't change again."

Bill-E waves a hand in front of his uncle's eyes — Dervish doesn't blink. He's crying when he looks at me. "I didn't want this!" he sobs. "I wanted to stop him from harming people, but not this way!"

"There was no other solution, short of killing him," I answer quietly. "Dervish had controlled the beast all these years, but it had grown stronger and was close to overwhelming him."

"And you don't know how long he'll be like this?" Bill-E asks.

I shake my head. "A week. A year. A decade. There's no telling."

Bill-E smiles weakly. "He must have really loved me to do this to himself," he notes proudly. "Only a father would act this selflessly."

I start to tell Bill-E the truth — that Dervish is his uncle, my dad was his dad, I'm his brother — then stop. What would it achieve? If I told him, he'd have to come to terms with his real dad's death and being an orphan. This way, he believes he's not alone. I think it's better to have a zombie for a father than no father at all.

"Yeah," I nod tiredly. "He was your dad. No doubt about it." Stepping forward, I take hold of one of Dervish's hands and press the other into Bill-E's. "Now let's get the hell out of here — this place gives me the creeps."

✠ Days.

Meera recovers the following afternoon. No memory loss or serious injury. I tell her the whole story while Bill-E's at home with Ma and Pa Spleen. She weeps when she sees Dervish. Cradles his face. Calls his name. Scours his eyes for a trace of who he was.

Nothing.

✠ Weeks.

Lawyers. Social workers. Bankers.

Meera goes through Dervish's drawers with me. Sets the bureaucratic wheels in motion. My world becomes a flurry of legal papers and professional advice. Concerned officials kept at bay by Dervish's lawyers. Regular inspections. Visits from doctors and welfare workers. Tests. Under observation. Having to prove myself capable of looking after both myself and my uncle.

Dervish isn't that difficult to care for. I lay out his clothes each night and dress him as soon as he wakes in the morning. He can go to the toilet himself, once I point him the right way. When I lead him down to breakfast, he sits and eats. After that he does whatever I tell him — rests, or exercises, or walks with me to the Vale to stock up on supplies and prove to everybody that he's healthy and unharmed. He's empty, distressingly so, and I have to spend a lot of time on him.

But I can cope.

✚ Months.
Autumn trundles round and I have to start school. Leaving Dervish alone in the house. I'm nervous the first few days, worrying about him, but when I realize he can't come to harm, I relax and settle down.

I sit next to Bill-E in most classes. (I've had to repeat a year, to make up for all the work I missed.) We get on better than ever. Occasionally he'll make mention of that night in the forest and cellar, but I always change the conversation quickly — I have no wish to dwell on such matters.

I enjoy school, and making friends — even homework! This is reality, the normal, dull, everyday world. It's great to be back.

✚ A year.
I grow four inches. Broaden. I was always large for my age — now I'm positively massive. And still growing! Bill-E

calls me the Impeccable Hulk, and refers to the two of us as Little and Large.

He spends a lot of weekends with Dervish and me, watching DVDs and MTV. He says we should hold a party and invite some girls over — says we could act like lords in a castle. Talks of getting a monocle for his lazy left eye and crowning himself King Bill-E the First. I just smile and say nothing when he starts up with fantasy stuff like that. Of course I'm interested in girls, but I'm not ready for dating yet. One step at a time. The demons were scary, but girls — well, girls are really terrifying!

Dervish hasn't changed. As lifeless as ever, eyes blank, never smiling or frowning, laughing or crying. I talk to him all the time, telling him about school, discussing TV shows, running math problems by him. He never shows any sign that he understands, but it's comforting to treat him like an ordinary person. And maybe, somewhere far away, in the midst of bloody battle, he hears — and perhaps it helps.

I take him to the barber's once a month, to have his hair and beard cut. Buy new clothes for him every so often. Experiment with various brands of deodorant. Keep him respectable and in shape, so if he ever does return, he won't have cause for complaint.

Meera drops by every few weeks or so. Keeps an eye on us. Drives me outside the Vale to hit the bigger stores. I tell her what Dervish said, about not leaving Carcery Vale, but she says it's OK as long as she's with me. But we're careful not to linger, always back a couple of hours before the sun sets — demons are more powerful in this world at night.

She usually sleeps over when she comes. Bill-E jokes about it and says we're having an affair. I wish!

I often dream of Lord Loss and his familiars. I worry about his threat and what he'll do to me if he ever gets the chance. I block the entrances to the secret cellar with thick planks and dozens of nails. Avoid Dervish's study as much as possible, for fear I'd find a book about Lord Loss, which might somehow allow him to latch onto me and break through Dervish's magic defences.

But even more than the demon master, I worry about *changing*. Every time a full moon comes I sleep nervously — if at all — tossing and turning, imagining the worst, checking under my nails first thing in the morning, examining my teeth and eyes in the mirror.

I've memorized the names and numbers of the Lambs — the Grady executioners. If I have to call them one day, I pray that I have the strength to do it.

✠ The morning after a full moon. Fourteen months since my battle with Lord Loss. A crisp, sun-crowned morning. Stretching. Yawning. Thinking about school. Also about a girl — Reni Gossel. I like Reni. Very cute. And she's been giving me the sort of looks that make me think she maybe thinks I'm cute too. Wondering if it's time to hold that party Bill-E's been pressing for.

My cheeks feel sticky. Curious, I rub a few fingers over them. They come away wet — and *red!*

My head flares. Heart pounds. Stomach clenches. Thoughts of school and Reni forgotten. I fall out of bed. Desperately check under my nails — dirty with earth and blood. Hairs stuck to my hands and around my mouth.

Moaning. Slapping off the hairs.

I reel out of the room and down the stairs, almost falling and breaking my neck. Head spinning. Lights exploding within my brain. Vomit rising in my throat. Telephone numbers flash across my eyes. "And the wolf shall lie down with the lamb."

Into the kitchen. Dervish is sitting at the table, slowly spooning corn flakes into his mouth. I turn in circles, wringing my hands, tearing at my hair. My eyes fix on the telephone hanging from the wall. I stop panicking. Calm falls on me like a sudden cold rainfall. I know what I must do. Best to do it now, as soon as possible, before I lose my nerve. Call the executioners. Give myself over to the Lambs. Arrange for others to take care of Dervish. Bid this world farewell.

I start towards the phone, resigned to my fate.

A solemn voice behind me — "Grubbs."

I turn slowly, reluctantly, for some reason expecting to see Lord Loss. But there's only Dervish. He's holding up a tin of red paint, a small pot of dirt, and a ratty woollen scarf that has been ripped into hairy fragments.

"The look on your face!" my uncle says.

And grins.

The horrifying adventures continue in

DEMON THIEF

Book 2 in THE DEMONATA series

Coming April 2006

Turn the page for a sneak peek. . . .

INTO THE LIGHT

✠　✠　✠

PEOPLE think I'm crazy because I see lights. I've seen them all my life. Strange, multicolored patches of lights, swirling through the air. The patches are different sizes, some as small as a coin, others as big as a cereal box. All sorts of shapes — octagons, triangles, decagons. Some have thirty or forty sides. I don't know the name for a forty-sided shape. *Quadradecagon?*

No circles. All of the patches have at least two straight edges. There are a few with curves or semicircular bulges, but not many.

Every color imaginable. Some shine brightly, others glow dully. Occasionally a few of the lights pulse, but normally they don't. Just hang there, glowing.

For a long time I didn't know the lights were strange. I thought everybody saw them. I described them to Mom and Dad when I learned to speak, but they thought I was playing a game, seeking attention. It was only when I started school and spoke about the lights in class that it became an issue. My teacher, Miss Tyacke, saw that I wasn't making up stories, that I really believed in the lights.

Miss Tyacke called Mom in. Suggested I visit somebody better qualified to understand what the lights signified. But Mom's never had much time for psychiatrists. She thinks the brain can take good care of itself if left alone. She asked me to stop mentioning the lights at school, but otherwise she wasn't concerned.

I stopped talking about the lights when Mom told me to, but the damage had already been done. Word spread among the children — Kernel Fleck is *weird*. He's not one of us. Stay away from him.

I never made many friends after that.

✠ My name's Cornelius, but I couldn't say that when I was younger. The closest I could get was Kernel. Mom and Dad thought that was cute and started using it instead of my real name. It stuck, and now that's what everybody calls me.

I think some parents shouldn't be allowed to name their kids. There should be a committee to disallow names that will cause problems later. I mean, even without the lights, what chance did I have of fitting in with any normal crowd with a name like Kernel Fleck!

We live in a city. Mom's a university lecturer. Dad's an artist who also does some freelance teaching. (He actually spends more time teaching than drawing, but whenever anyone asks, he says he's an artist.) We live on the third floor of an old warehouse that has been converted into apartments. Huge rooms with very high ceilings. I sometimes feel like a Munchkin, or Jack in the giant's castle.

Dad's very good with his hands. He makes brilliant model airplanes and hangs them from the wooden beams in the ceiling of my bedroom. When they start to clutter the place up, or if we just get the urge one lazy Sunday afternoon, the two of us make bombs out of apples, conkers — whatever we can find that's hard and round — and launch them at the planes. We fire away until we run out of ammo or all the planes are destroyed. Then Dad sets to work on new models and the process gets repeated. At the moment, the ceiling's about a third full.

I like the city. Our house is great; we're close to lots of shops, a cool adventure playground, museums, cinemas galore. School's OK too. I don't make friends, but I like my teachers and the building — we have a first-rate lab, a projection room, a massive library. And I never get bullied — I roar automatically when I'm fighting, which isn't good news for bullies who don't want to attract attention!

But, sweet as life should be, I'm not happy. I feel lonely. I've always been a loner, but it didn't bother me when I was younger. I liked being my myself. I read lots of books and comics, watched dozens of TV shows, invented imaginary friends to play with. I was content.

That changed recently. I don't know why, but I don't like being alone now. I feel sad when I see groups of friends having a good time. I want to be part of them. I want friends who'll tell me jokes and laugh at mine, who I can discuss television shows and music with, who'll pick me to be in their teams. I try getting people to accept me, but the harder I try, the more they avoid me. I sometimes hover at the edge of a group, ignored, and pretend I'm part of it. But if I speak, it backfires. They glare at me suspiciously, move away, or tell me to get lost. "Go watch some lights, freak!"

The loneliness began maybe three or four months ago, but got really bad this last month. I'm not enjoying life anymore. The hours drag, especially at home or when I have free time at school. I can't distract myself. My mind wanders. I keep thinking about friends and how I don't have any, that I'm alone and might always be this way. I've talked with Mom and Dad about it, as much as I can, but it's hard to make them see how miserable I am. They said things would change when I was older, but I don't believe them. I'll still be weird, no matter how old I am. Why should people like me more then than now?

I try so hard to fit in. I watch the popular shows and listen to the bands I hear others talking about. I read all the hot comics and books. Wear cool clothes when I'm not at school. Use all the latest slang and curses.

It doesn't matter. Nothing works. Nobody likes me. I'm wasting my time. This past week, I've gotten to thinking that I'm wasting my entire life. I've had dark, horrible thoughts, where I can see only one way out, one way of stopping the pain and loneliness. I know it's wrong to think that way — life can never be *that* bad — but it's hard not to. I cry when I'm alone — once or twice I've even cried in class. I'm eating too much food, putting on weight. I've stopped washing and my skin's gotten greasy. I don't care. I want to look like the freak I feel I am.

✠ Late at night. In bed. Playing with the patches of light, trying not to think about the loneliness. I've always been able to play with the lights. I remember being three or four years old, the lights all around me, reaching out and moving them, trying to fit them together like jigsaw pieces. Normally the lights remain at a distance of several feet or more, but I can call them closer when I want.

The patches aren't solid. They're like floating scraps of plastic. If I look at a patch from the side, it's almost invisible. I can put my fingers through them, like ordinary pools of light. But, despite all that, I can move them around.

When I want to move a patch, I focus on it and it glides towards me, stopping when I tell it. Reaching out, I push at one of the edges with my fingers. There's no contact, but as my fingers get closer, the light moves in whatever direction I'm pushing. When I stop, the light stops. I figured out very early on that I could put patches together to make mosaic-like shapes. I've been doing it ever since, at night, or during lunch at school when I have nobody to play with. Playing with them more than ever recently. Sometimes the lights are the only way I have to escape the miserable loneliness for a while.

I like making weird shapes, like Pablo Picasso paintings. I saw a program on him at school a couple of years ago, and felt an immediate connection. I think Picasso saw lights too, only he didn't tell anyone. People wouldn't think he was a great artist if he'd said he saw lights — they'd say he was a nutcase, like me.

The shapes I make are nowhere near as fabulous as Pablo Picasso's paintings. I'm no artist. I just try to create interesting patterns that will amuse me. They're rough, but I like them. They never last either. The shapes hold as long as I'm studying them, but once I lose interest or fall asleep, they come undone and the pieces drift apart, returning to their original positions in the air around me.

The one I'm making tonight is particularly jumbled. I'm finding it hard to concentrate. Joining the pieces randomly, not making any real shape. It's a mess. I can't stop thinking about friends and not having any. Feeling wretched. Wishing I had at least one true friend, someone who'd care about me and play with me, so I wouldn't be completely alone in this big, scary world.

As I'm thinking about that, and getting ready to move on from the lights, a few of the patches pulse. Just a handful, in different places. No big deal. Lights have pulsed before, from time to time. Usually I ignore them. But tonight, sad and desperate to divert my train of thought, I summon a couple, study them with a frown, then put them together and call for the rest of the flashing patches. As I add those pieces to the first two, more lights pulse, some slowly, some quickly.

Sitting up, working with more speed. Interested in this new, flashing shape. I've never put pulsing patches together. Adding to the cluster, more lights pulsing as the piece takes shape. I put them in place almost without thought, on auto-pilot. It's like the way I roar when I'm fighting — I have no control over it. I keep watching for a pattern to emerge, but there isn't one. Just a mass of different, pulsing colors. Still, it's worked its magic. I'm focused on the cluster of lights now, dark thoughts and fears temporarily forgotten.

The lights build and build. A massive structure, much larger than any I've created before. I'm sweating, and my arms are aching. I want to stop and rest, but I can't. I'm almost obsessed with the pulsing lights. This must be what addiction is like. We had a couple of police officers come in to speak to our class last term. They told us about the dangers of becoming an addict, all the things that . . .

Without warning, the patches that I've stuck together stop pulsing and glow the same light blue color. I fall back from this new, uniform patch, gasping, as if I'd gotten an electric shock. I've never seen this happen. It scares me. A huge, blue, jagged patch of light at the foot of my bed. Large enough for a person to fit through.

My first thought is to flee, call for Mom and Dad, get out as quick as I can. But part of me holds firm. An inner voice whispers in my ear, telling me to stay. *This is your window to a life of wonders,* it says. *But be careful,* it adds, as I move closer to the light. *Windows open both ways.*

As it says that, a shape presses through, out of the panel of light. I'm too horrified to scream. It's a monster from my very worst nightmare. Pale red skin. A pair of dark red eyes. No nose. A small mouth. Sharp, grey teeth. As it leans farther forward, into my bedroom, its chest becomes visible, and the horror intensifies. It doesn't have a heart! There's a hole in the left side of its chest, and inside the hole — dozens of tiny, hissing snakes.

The monster frowns and stretches out a hand towards me. I can see more than two arms — at least four or five. I want to pull away. Dive beneath my bed. Scream for help. But the voice that spoke to me a few seconds ago won't let me. It whispers quickly, words I can't follow. And I find myself standing firm, taking a step towards the panel of light and its emerging monster. I raise my right hand and watch the fingers curl into a fist. There's a strange tingling sensation in my fingers, like pins and needles.

The monster stops. Its eyes narrow. It looks around my bedroom uncertainly. Then, slowly, smoothly, it withdraws, pulling back into the panel of light, vanishing from the chest upwards, until only its red eyes remain, staring out at me from within the surrounding blueness, twin circles of an unspoken evil. Then they're gone too, and I'm alone again, just me and the light.

I should be wailing for help, running for my life, cowering on the floor. But all that happens is my fingers relax and my fist un-clenches. I'm facing the panel of blue light, staring at it like a zombie fixed on the sight of a fresh human brain, distantly processing information. Normally I can see objects through the patches of light, but I can't see through this. If I look around it, there's my bedroom wall, a chest of drawers, toys and socks scattered around the floor. But when I look directly at the light, blue is all I see.

The voice says something crazy to me. I know it's madness as soon as it speaks. I want to argue, roar at it, tell it to get stuffed. But, as scared and confused as I am, I can't hold myself back. I find my legs tensing. I know, with sick certainty, what's going to happen next. I open my mouth to scream, to try to stop it, but before I can, a force makes me step forward — after the monster, into the light.